Famous Tales From Britain

With Activities for the Primary Classroom

Barry Nicholson

Starhands Publishing

Famous Tales From Britain: Locations

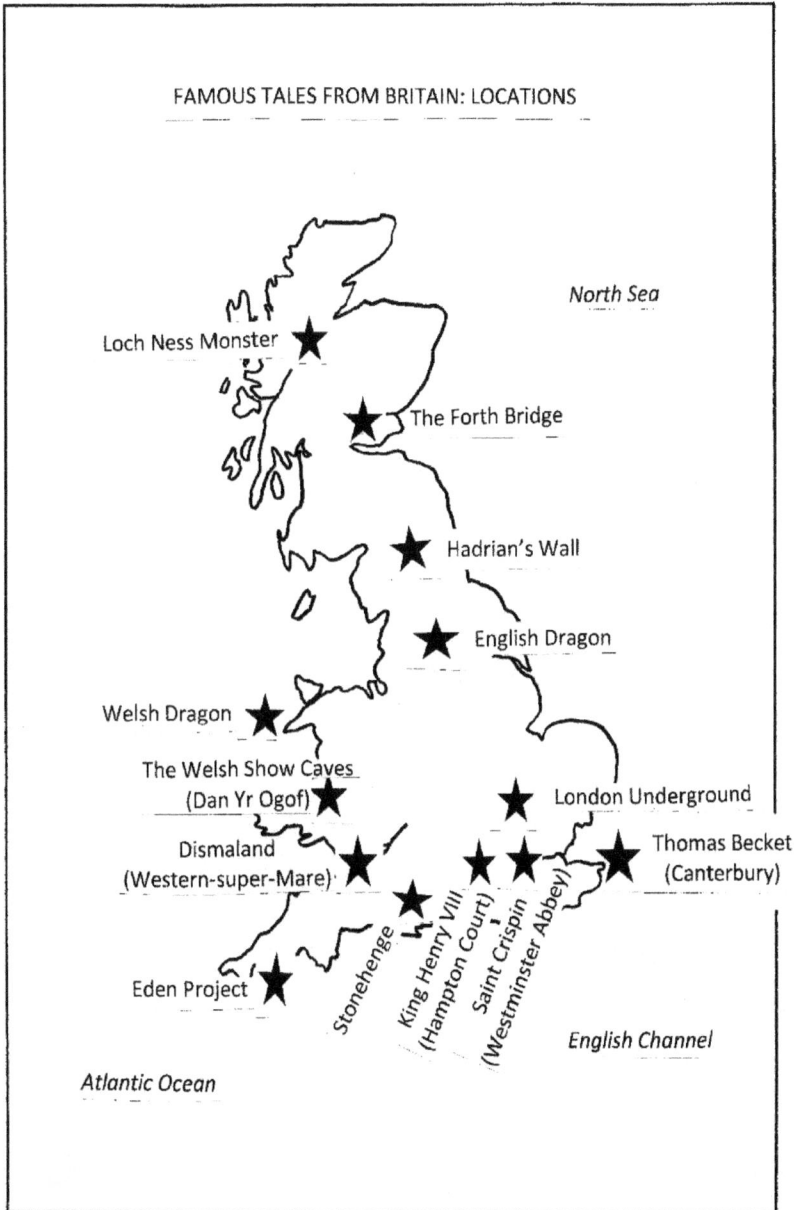

FAMOUS TALES FROM BRITAIN: LOCATIONS

North Sea

Loch Ness Monster

The Forth Bridge

Hadrian's Wall

English Dragon

Welsh Dragon

The Welsh Show Caves
(Dan Yr Ogof)

London Underground

Dismaland
(Western-super-Mare)

Thomas Becket
(Canterbury)

Stonehenge

King Henry VIII
(Hampton Court)

Saint Crispin
(Westminster Abbey)

Eden Project

English Channel

Atlantic Ocean

BARRY NICHOLSON

CONTENTS

CONTENTS

LIST OF ACTIVITIES

BARRY NICHOLSON

INTRODUCTION

Most of us have heard of the Loch Ness Monster, Henry VIII, and the London Underground, but how about Banksy's Dismaland, The Eden Project, or Saint Crispin? They are all from this green, pleasant and often chaotic land called Great Britain, and provide a rich tapestry of tale and intrigue.

Britain is an ancient land, with conquests by the Romans and Normans; the country gave rise to the industrial revolution and has also seen the depths of world war. From the most northerly point on the mainland at John O'Groats in Scotland to its most southerly point at Land's End in Cornwall measures 874 miles by road; between these two places lie many tales of history, mystery and personality.

This book has been written with children in mind. Children love tales of legend and mystery, especially when connected with historical characters or animals. Within these pages you will find a wealth of interesting and intriguing characters, both human and animal. Add to that some impressive architecture and the remains of ancient cultures and you have a recipe for success.

I like the idea of this book because it links legends and tales from Britain to actual practical activities for the classroom. I think that this is the primary strength of the book: it turns the academic into the practical, the intangible asset of a cultural story or tale into a real-life and concrete end result. The idea of turning theory into practice is especially important for teaching children, who often need a concrete visualisation of a tale or legend so that it sticks in their minds and they learn from it.

That's why there are suggested activities at the end of each chapter. Some of the activities are academic, some are games, some involve drawing or colouring, or maybe a speaking activity such as a role-play. The aim is to try to give the tales a 3D feel, to bring them to life, and create engagement with the children. Each activity is different, and their purpose is to suggest to the teacher or parent a method of extending the tale into the real world. Some of the activities challenge the children's creative and artistic capability. One is a quiz about comparatives and superlatives. Another challenges the children to design their own set of coins.

There are twelve chapters in this book and each focusses on a tale or set of tales, often with some kind of moral. The twelve chapters are:

- *The Loch Ness Monster*: If we are to believe the various photos, films, sonar records and sightings then there really is a dinosaur-style monster in the depths of Loch Ness;
- *King Henry VIII and his Six Wives*: Henry VII is known for his succession of wives, some of whom met a deadly fate and return from time to time as ghosts;
- *The Forth Bridge*: Completed in 1890 and an engineering marvel, it became a UNESCO World Heritage Site in 2015 and gives rise to the saying "it's like painting the Forth Bridge";
- *The London Underground*: The oldest underground railway system in the world celebrated its 150th anniversary in 2013 and its bullseye motif and stylised map design have become iconic symbols;
- *The Welsh Show Caves*: Many carboniferous limestone caves 'lurk' beneath the Brecon Beacons National Park, and some of them are accessible around Dan Yr Ogof;
- *Thomas Becket*: The murder of Thomas Becket remains one of the most important events of Medieval England, and shows how two friends can become enemies with catastrophic results;

- *St. Crispin's Day*: It is memorable for the many battles that occurred on that day, notably of Agincourt in 1415 in which Shakespeare's Henry V speaks the famous lines "We few, we happy few, we band of brothers";
- *Hadrian's Wall: Wall of Empire*: One of the greatest structures of the Roman Empire is Hadrian's Wall, stretching 118km and marking the northern boundary of the Roman Empire;
- *A Tale of Two Dragons:* Taking their place in mythology are two important British dragons: the poisonous dragon that Saint George killed, and the proud Welsh dragon;
- *Stonehenge: Circles in Stone*: People flock to the prehistoric circle, but wrangling over the site and a lack of facilities have left visitors wondering if there is really much for them to see;
- *Banksy's Dismaland*: Banksy is a British street artist whose art is urban and graffiti inspired. His latest work is a theme park that is dreary and dismal on purpose;
- *The Eden Project*: This award-winning attraction is designed to show the relationship of humanity with the plant and biological world, housed within space-age domes and gardens.

I have personally been to a lot of the sites in this book, and most are accessible by public transport. Some information came from these site visits, but much of the material has come from books or from the internet, and a final section gives credit to the various sources. Check out these references if you'd like any more details in addition to what I present here.

And, of course, don't forget to create materials and ideas of your own!

Barry Nicholson
London 2016

1.
LOCH NESS MONSTER: REAL OR FAKE?

1.
LOCH NESS MONSTER: REAL OR FAKE?

If we are to believe the various photos, films, sonar records and sightings then there really is a dinosaur-style monster in the depths of Loch Ness.

The loch (Scottish for lake) is around twenty two and a half miles long and one and a half miles wide, and runs to a depth of 754 feet (229.8 metres). It holds around 16,430,000 gallons of water and is thus the largest body of fresh water in Britain. The River Ness is the only outlet to the open sea flowing seven miles through Inverness into the Moray Firth. It is thus perfect habitat for a variety of creatures – including ours.

The Cambridge Online Dictionary defines a monster as "an imaginary frightening creature, especially one that is large and strange".

Our 'monster' is called Nessie and belongs to a family known as cryptid with a sub-grouping as a lake monster. Accounts typically put the monster as between four to nine metres long, with one claim at thirty metres long. Commonly the animal has a small head, though there have been sightings of large flat head and neck four or five metres long, or even a horned gargoyle head. Its neck is slightly thicker than an elephant's trunk, and its body resembles a plesiosaur. Some describe the body as large and thick or even lumpy; protrusions at the bottom of the creature's body could be flippers or legs. Two or three humps have been seen to rise out of the water, the largest of which is around fifty feet in length. Its three metre tail is flattened and highly flexible. The animal can walk aswell as swim, crossing roads in front of drivers and onlookers, lurching like a seal. It has also variously been likened to an otter, a giant marine worm, an eel, or an elephant squid (complete with trunk and eye), and most often plesiosaur-like.

There are also descriptions of its movement: splashing and diving, turbulent swishing of its tail surrounded in a flurry of bubbles, rolling and plunging in the water with considerable commotion and a plume of spray. Some say that it has the appearance of 'two fighting ducks'. Most say that it moves fast like a speedboat, sometimes with long bursts of movement. On one occasion it kept pace with a fast expedition boat that was tracking it with sonar.

Nessie is often spoken of as a solitary animal, but if it exists there must be many of them, at least two, or more likely a family of them. In biological terms, there must be dozens or even hundreds of them to sustain a breeding population. However, looking at the food chain in the loch there is not enough to feed a population of plesiosaurs, and that's including fish, eels and catfish.

Sightings of the Loch Ness Monster pre-1933 were rare, but I have been able to locate three. The very first record is of Saint Columba, an Irish monk who was visiting the area in 565. He came across some locals burying a man on the banks of the River Ness. He had been attacked and dragged under by a 'waterbeast' whilst swimming in the river. Columba sent one of his followers to swim across the river and the beast came after him too. Columba made the sign of the cross and commanded it to "go back at once" at which the monster retreated. Moving on to 1650, the English army were trying to gain more control over the Highland clans. They built a large ship that was docked in the lock for this purpose. The writer, Richard Franck, was on board the ship and wrote of 'floating islands' of peat and vegetation that massed in the lock that could easily be misidentified as monsters. Thirdly, in 1871-2, Dr D. Mackenzie saw an object like a log or upturned boat "wriggling and churning up the water" and moved at a fast speed.

Modern interest skyrocketed in the 1930s with a number of famous sightings and photographs, and since that time a whole stream of evidence has come forward. How we interpret these is up to us, but the wealth of 'evidence' does seem to point to / suggest the existence of some sort of creature.

Let's leave historical evidence and sightings behind and look at some modern sightings since 1933 and examine the evidence for and against the existence of the monster with the primary question: is the Loch Ness Monster real or fake?

Real: the evidence:

The sheer number of sightings is surely evidence enough, some of them quite by chance and others the result of expeditions and scientific study.

The most convincing photograph was taken on the 19th April 1934 by Robert Kenneth Wilson, a London doctor, in what has become known as the surgeon's photograph. He was fowl shooting in the Highlands with a friend when they noticed a 'considerable commotion' as something broke the surface about 200 yards away. Wilson's friend shouted "my god, it's the monster!", and Wilson himself had time to take just four photos before it disappeared back into the water. Only two of the photos came out which he sold to the *Daily Mail*. One of the two photos became the iconic 'neck and head' photo.

Dinsdale, who himself has claimed to have seen the monster, says that the photo is no hoax: he notes that ripples behind the neck as the animal broke the surface point to a larger part of the animal that is underwater. The surgeon's photo is widely regarded as good evidence of the existence of the monster, and is a good example of an eyewitness report backed up by photos.

Other evidence includes Stuart's 1951 'hump' photo and Edwards's 2011 photo; cine camera and video evidence includes Dinsdale 1960 and Holmes 2007; sonar evidence provided by Operation Deepscan 1987; and Apple Maps 2014 satellite evidence of a 'mysterious shape' reported in the *Daily Mail*, the most recent positive evidence. The *Daily Mail* article writes of a 'shadowy form' of about thirty metres (100ft) powered by two giant flippers. Apparently it looks like a boat wake, but the boat is missing. The image was spotted on one of Apple's smartphone maps of the area by eagle-eyed users and forwarded to the Official Loch Ness Monster Fan Club who in turn welcomed the use of satellite technology to locate the monster. The club's president, Mr Campbell, said the images were "likely" to be the elusive beast.

Fake: the evidence:

Sceptics have a lot of ammunition at their disposal, and it is easy to see their side of the story.

Many of the sightings have turned out to be hoaxes, which is disappointing. The most famous example is the Surgeon's photo of 1934 (see above) which some claim to be an elaborate fake. The scale of the photo is put into question, as it is often cropped to make the monster seem larger and the waves surrounding it disproportionately large. In the original image it is clear that the water is in ripples, not large waves. The documentary *Loch Ness Discovered* (1993) found a man-made 'object', 60-90 cm long, to be the cause of the ripples as it was towed across the loch.

Surgeon's photo was proved a fake in an article in *The Sunday Telegraph* in December 1975, and details emerged in 1999 about how the 'monster' was actually an adapted toy submarine bought from Woolworth's!

This lack of conclusive evidence is backed up by the BBC's 2003 study *Searching for the Loch Ness Monster* that failed to find any animal of any size despite the use of sonar beams and satellite tracking. The study searched "from shoreline to shoreline, top to bottom" and concluded that Nessie is "only a myth".

There is a lot of debate about misidentification, as what people have seen might actually have been examples of animals that normally live in the habitat. Nessie could in fact be a giant eel, and conger eels are known to live in the loch. Eels can grow to great sizes, especially in length, and can appear to look as sea serpents in the right light. Against this is that eels cannot protrude from the water like a neck and head, and in fact move from side to side, unlike Nessie's humps that soar out of the water. Seals are another explanation, and are also known to live in the loch. Long-necked seals were reported in Sir Edward Mountain's expedition in 1934, and it is known that a grey seal has a surprisingly long neck, is of similar colour, and has been seen 'crossing the road' from time to time.

Though elephants are not a normal animal in the habitat, it has been put forward as a possible explanation. Power and Johnson (1979) claimed that the Surgeon's photograph was in fact a swimming elephant, and that the photo was taken elsewhere and claimed to be taken on the loch. It has also been suggested that there were in fact elephants in the loch from a travelling circus. In either case the elephant's trunk could be the head and neck, and its head and back the humps.

Other inanimate misidentifications have included trees and logs, and waves and wakes. Dr Maurice Burton (1982) claimed that the shape of logs resemble descriptions of the monster. The 'gargoyle head' noted earlier is one such example of an oddly-shaped tree stump or log. Apparently the fermenting logs of scots pine trees occasionally float to the surface and can appear monster-like. Boat wakes have also been cited as possible explanations for Nessie sightings: a boat's wake divides and hits both sides of the loch, then the deflecting waves meet back in the middle causing a 'standing wave' of a humped appearance. Could this be mistaken for a monster?

Finally, a lot of descriptions are vague, of a 'dark object' of 'considerable size', a 'very large creature' even just a 'shape' in the water. One account does not describe the monster at all, just its 'mysterious wave' as it moves through the water. Add to this that many of the photos are inconclusive, murky or pixelated. Gray's photo of 1933, for example, is the only one of five photos taken to come out during developing; Sir Edward Mountain's (1934) expedition revealed only five photos, four of which were clearly made by boat wakes and the fifth only showing 'an isolated area of disturbance with spray'. A short 16mm film made on the same expedition showed nothing much as, typically, the distance from the object had been too great. These objects and shapes can easily be confused with animals commonly found in the area such as otters or seals: we simply don't know.

What does it look like? Does it have flippers? Does it have a tail? Does it have a long neck? Or does it exist at all? How can an animal so large be seen so infrequently, timidly showing itself from place to place and year to year? As D Lowrance of *Operation Deepscan* (1987) said, "There's something here that we don't understand, and there's something there that's larger than a fish, maybe some species that hasn't been detected before. I don't know".

My opinion is that Nessie exists, but I also acknowledge that there are some vagaries and difficult questions to answer that can be easily magnified by the sceptic. Surely there is something there, even if the monster exists only as an abstract noun – a myth – which, over decades, has manifested itself as reality. Who knows? If you want something enough you might just get it!

Loch Ness is situated between Fort William and Inverness in the Highlands of Scotland and is best accessed by private car or on a tour. The A82 connects these two places, and runs for much of its length along the northern shore of the loch. To the north are the Northern Highlands and to the south the Grampian Mountains. Loch Ness is north of Scotland's highest peak, Ben Nevis. By train it is possible to reach the area by train from Edinburgh or Glasgow to Inverness, and then south by bus or tour. It is a very remote area and will take some time and patience to get to – but then that's why Nessie chose to live here.

Online there is countless information on Loch Ness and the history of expeditions and sightings. Loch Ness is also on Google Street View, allowing the user to look both above and below the surface of the lake.

The hotels and restaurants in the area are well versed in Nessie information and the needs of Nessie-hunters and offer a range of guidebooks, maps, and colouring books for children. Evidently the existence of a monster is good for business. The tour companies sell from the 'tale and legend' angle rather than promising trippers will see the monster itself, probably wise considering the chances of seeing the beast are fairly low. One example of a tour company is *Loch Ness by Jacobite* who offer nine cruise options including a Full Loch Ness Cruise with live sonar on board to watch out for Nessie. With a focus on myth, tale and legend, of what *might* be or what you *might* see, this kind of intangible cultural tourism is limitless!

As a final note Steve Feltham (in *The Times*, 16th July 2015), a life-long fan and supporter of Nessie, officially concluded that the creature is a catfish! In 1991 Feltham gave up his girlfriend, house and job to devote his life to looking for the beast, but has now given up his true love: Nessie. He now says that it is a European Wels Catfish, that can grow up to four meters long, and has a long, curved back fitting many of the descriptions. He concludes "I have to be honest. I just don't think that Nessie is a prehistoric monster".

What do you think? Is Nessie real or fake? Would you like to go on a 'monster expedition' to find Nessie?

Idea for the Classroom: Comparative and Superlative Quiz

Nessie is arguably the most famous monster in the world, but what do you know about other highest, fastest, longest and heaviest in the world? Test your own knowledge and that of your students with this quiz, designed to be played in teams.

Animals

What is the largest animal in the world? *(The blue whale)*
What is the fastest animal in the world? *(The cheetah)*
How fast can a tiger run: 26, 36, 46 or 56 kmh? *(56)*
Penguins can swim faster than humans. True or false? *(True)*

Countries

What is the largest country in the world? *(Russia)*
What is the smallest country in the world? *(The Vatican City)*
What is the capital of Australia? *(Canberra)*
Who was the first president of the US? *(George Washington)*

Rivers & Mountains

What is the longest river in the world? *(The Nile)*
What is the highest mountain in Scotland? *(Ben Nevis)*
Which is the highest waterfall in the world? *(Angel Falls, Venezuela, at 3,281 feet)*
Where is the largest active volcano in the world? *(Mauna Loa, Hawaii, at 13,650 feet)*

People

Who is the richest person in the world? *(The Sultan of Brunei)*
Where is the singer Kylie Minogue from? *(Australia)*
When did Alexander Graham Bell invent the telephone: 1875, 1895 or 1925? *(1875)*
What country has the largest population in the world? *(China)*

Crazy World Records

When was the Guinness Book of Records first published: 1945, 1955 or 1965? *(1955)*
How old was the oldest person: 122, 132 or 142? *(122)*
Which is the biggest city in the world? *(Mexico City)*
What was the world's fastest passenger plane? *(Concorde)*

Idea for the Classroom: Wanted Poster

Wanted! One large plesiosaur, located somewhere in Loch Ness, reward $1,000! Using the example below as a guide, create your own *Nessie: Wanted* poster. You never know, it may lead you to the real thing! Don't forget to include information on your monster's name, home, when it was first seen, description, personality, family, and the reward.

Idea for the Classroom: True or False?

The legend of the Loch Ness Monster has been around for a long time, and various evidence has emerged both for and against its existence. Are we dealing with a real-life plesiosaur or at a bunch of hoaxes and fiction? Look at the statements below. Are these statements true or false? What do you think? Some of the answers are in the text above and others you have to guess.

1. The first alleged sighting of the monster was in the year 565. *True or false?*
2. The BBC's 2003 study *Searching for the Loch Ness Monster* found the monster. *True or false?*
3. Gray (1933) took five photos but only one came out. *True or false?*
4. There is more water in Loch Ness than all the other lakes in England, Scotland and Wales put together. *True or false?*
5. The only outlet to the open sea is the River Ness. *True or False?*
6. Loch Ness never freezes – there is too much water and it is too deep. *True or false?*
7. One tour company guarantees that you will see Nessie. *True or false?*
8. Nessie has wings and can fly. *True or false?*
9. Mr Feltham gave up his girlfriend, house and job to go searching for the monster. *True or false?*
10. The Loch Ness monster really exists. *True or false?*

Answers: 1T 2F 3T 4T 5T 6T 7F 8F 9T 10?

Wanted Poster

WANTED

Loch Ness Monster

nickname: Nessie
home: Loch Ness, Scotland
first seen: AD 565
description: long neck, humped back, flippers
personality: shy, evades detection or capture
family: other dinosaurs

Reward $1,000

BARRY NICHOLSON

2.
HENRY VIII
AND HIS
SIX WIVES

2.
KING HENRY VIII
AND HIS
SIX WIVES

King Henry VIII is known for his succession of wives, some of whom met a deadly fate and return from time to time as ghosts.

Henry's favourite seat was at Hampton Court Palace in Surrey. He took over and extended Cardinal Wolsey's Tudor building, creating a palace truly fit for a king. His greatest architectural order was the Great Hall, completed in 1536. It is 106 feet long, 40 feet wide, and 60 feet high (32.3×12.1×18.2 metres). Henry held banquets here, sitting at the high table (one step above floor level) whilst his guests sat at tables ranged along the main walls.

At Hampton Court he had around 500 servants; at the top of the household were the Lord Steward, Lord Treasurer, Astronomer Royal, priests, secretaries and physicians. At the bottom were cup bearers, yeomen, ushers, pages, cooks and grooms.

Despite the fact that the palace was well-guarded, Henry was well aware of possible threats to his crown and to himself. Each night a small army of servants prepared and searched Henry's bed, probing the straw on which Henry's mattress lay with a dagger to ensure nothing was concealed; at mealtimes he had tasters to ensure his food and drink was not poisoned. Apparently he could be generous if he liked someone but dangerous if he did not. This is something his six wives were to find out.

His greatest wish was to produce a son and heir, and this reason alone led to the failure of many of his marriages. He was married to his first wife, Katherine of Aragon, for twenty-four years, and they had a daughter (later Mary I). But Henry wanted a son, and so divorced her after she became too old to bear children. He had to persuade the Pope to accept the divorce, and this produced a deep rift between Henry and the Pope.

He took Anne Boleyn as his mistress, then wife, and moved to Hampton Court with her, and set about enlarging the palace: another gallery, library, study, kitchens, tennis court and wine cellar. They also produced a daughter (later Elizabeth I) which angered Henry who expected a son. This, together with her unlucky gambling, led to her demise. Accused of adultery, she was sent to the Tower of London and on 19th May 1536 she was beheaded.

Soon after appeared Jane Seymour, for whom he furnished new apartments at Hampton Court. Ten days after Anne's beheading he married Jane, who on 12th October 1537 gave birth to a son (later Edward VI). This, of course, made Henry very happy but this was short-lived as Jane became very ill and her strength disappeared. Twelve days after the birth she died.

Henry married and divorced his fourth wife, Anne of Cleves, very quickly. He had been told of the twenty-four year old's attractiveness, and so on New Year's day 1540 he sailed down the Thames to Rochester to meet Anne and her ship. Unfortunately he did not like the look of his new bride-to-be, but the marriage contract was set in place. Days after the marriage their divorce was approved.

In 1540 he married wife number five, Catherine Howard, and at first the marriage went well. However, Henry increasingly felt that she had nothing much to offer him and, noting elicit sexual relations with other men, had her beheaded at the Tower on 10th February 1542.

His final wife was Kateryn Parr, aged thirty-one, who he married in 1543. By now Henry was in old age, and her affectionate and domestic manner was more suited to his age and temperament. She outlived him: Henry VIII died at Westminster Palace on 28th January 1547 with the famous words "All is lost!".

Do some of Henry VIII's wives still 'live' as ghosts? Apparently so. There have been several spooky sightings of Jane Seymour, Henry's third wife who died in childbirth in 1537. A tall lady dressed in white with a long train and a smiling face, and lighted taper, she glides around Clock Court, the Queens' Old Apartments and the Silver Stick Gallery. She has been seen to pass through closed doors and glide up and down stairs.

After her grisly fate at the Tower in 1542, Catherine Howard has been sighted many times in the Haunted Gallery, named after her famous ghost. Ugly rumours had begun to circulate about her un-Royal behaviour with other men and so Henry had her held as prisoner in her room at the palace awaiting her removal to the Tower. She managed to break free and run along the gallery in an effort to plead for her life with her husband. However, Henry, who was celebrating mass in the chapel, paid no attention to her. She was held by the guards who dragged her back to her room shrieking and sobbing for mercy. Her 'piercing scream' could be heard all over the palace.

Underwood (1971) notes the location as the Queen's Great Staircase from which a low-roofed corridor can be seen; it contains the room from which Catherine escaped and to which she was dragged back.

The shadowy image of a woman in a white gown has been seen near the door to the Royal pew in the chapel. The image vanishes suddenly to the sound of a blood-chilling scream. The shrieking figure runs through the Haunted Gallery on the night of the anniversary.

Residents in the palace's grace and favour apartments have reported being awakened in the night by shrieks that seemed to come from the Haunted Gallery. The most recent sighting was in 1945 by a resident, Mr. Irwin. He saw a female in strange dress walking around the palace gardens at noon; a waiter who overheard his conversation remarked that Catherine had been "walking a great deal lately".

Finally, Anne Boleyn, another victim of beheading, was also reportedly seen in the Haunted Gallery in the late 1800s. Dressed in blue, she surprised a servant who recognised her from a portrait in the palace.

What do you make of all this? It might be an idea to go and look for yourself. Hampton Court is a very popular tourist destination with prices to match. It is in south-west London and is easy to get to by train to Hampton Court station (from London Waterloo) or local bus from Richmond (R68) or Kingston (111, 216, 411, 461). The train and some of the buses drop you off on the other side of the River Thames, making for a pleasant walk across Hampton Court Bridge to get to the main entrance at Trophy Gate. From April to September there are also river boats from Westminster, Richmond and Kingston: fake paddle steamers in true Mississippi style.

The front and side gardens are free of charge, as are the rear gardens out of season. If you'd like to enter the palace itself then be prepared for an eye-watering charge to get in. It might be cheaper to join a tour arranged with a central London operator. Should you require refreshment there is no shortage of cafes, bars and restaurants in the surrounding area, especially in Bridge Road near Hampton Court station. If you have a thin wallet then a packed lunch is a better option.

In 2015 leaflets and posters invited you to "come and celebrate 500 years of drama", as Hampton court's 500th anniversary was celebrated. Special events were held daily from April to December.

Idea for the Classroom: Written Questions

Answer the questions in written form. All answers are below.

a) Answer the questions:
1. Henry VIII had three children. Who were they?
2. Two of Henry's wives were beheaded. Who were they?
3. Which of his wives died in childbirth?
4. Which of his wives outlived him?
5. What were Henry VIII's last words?
6. Whose ghost is said to give a 'piercing scream'?
7. Whose ghost was dressed in blue?

b) Put the words into the correct order to make sentences:
1. six wives Henry VIII had.
2. 1536 the Great Hall completed was in.
3. 1542 the Tower sent was to in Catherine Howard.
4. attraction tourist Hampton Court a is popular.
5. ghost glides Jane Seymour's Clock around Court.
6. 500 years celebrate and come drama of.
7. www.hrp.org.uk found information more can be at.

c) Here is a list of Henry VIII's six wives. Put them in order, add dates, and tell of their fate:

wife	married from...	until...	fate	Is there a ghost?
Anne Boleyn				
Anne of Cleves				
Kateryn Parr				
Catherine Howard				
Katherine of Aragon				
Jane Seymour				

d) Fill the gaps with the correct information:

    1. Henry VIII ordered the construction of the Great Hall in 1536. Its measurements are _____ by _____ by _____.

    2. Guests sat at tables ranged along the walls whilst Henry sat at the _____, one step above floor level.

    3. At Hampton Court he had around _____ servants.

    4. Henry VIII died on _____ at _____ with the words " _____ ".

    5. River boats run to Hampton Court from _____, _____ and _____.

    6. In 2015 Hampton Court celebrates its _____ anniversary.

    7. My favourite of Henry's wives is _____ because _____.

e) Free writing: You are a guest of Henry VIII visiting Hampton Court Palace, and you are amazed at the rooms and decoration. Imagine and describe what you can see, and write descriptions of:

- The Great Hall *(high ceiling, decorated walls...)*
- A royal banquet *(many tables, food and drink...)*
- The Library *(bookcases, books, reading tables...)*
- The Kitchens & Wine Cellar *(smell, cooking, cooks...)*

You may need to do some research in books or on the internet to find pictures of these places. Start your description like this:

"I visited Hampton Court Palace today and I saw some amazing things..."

Answers:

a) 1 Mary, Elizabeth, Edward 2 Anne Boleyn, Catherine Howard 3 Jane Seymour 4 Kateryn Parr 5 All is lost! 6 Catherine Howard 7 Anne Boleyn

b)

wife	married from...	until...	fate	Is there a ghost?
Katherine of Aragon	1509	1533	divorced	no
Anne Boleyn	1533	1536	beheaded	yes
Jane Seymour	1536	1537	died in childbirth	yes
Anne of Cleves	1540	1540	divorced	no
Catherine Howard	1540	1542	beheaded	yes
Kateryn Parr	1543	1547	outlived him	no

c) 1 Henry VII had six wives. 2 The Great Hall was completed in 1536. 3 Catherine Howard was sent to the tower in 1542. 4 Hampton Court is a popular tourist attraction. 5 Jane Seymour's ghost glides around Clock Court. 6 Come and celebrate 500 years of drama. 7 More information can be found at www.hrp.org.uk.

d) 1 106ft, 40ft, 60ft 2 high table 3 500 4 28th January 1547, Westminster Palace, All is lost! 5 Westminster, Richmond, Kingston 6 500 year / 500th 7 ?

e) For example:

> *"I visited Hampton Court Palace today and saw some amazing things. The Great Hall was large and had golden decorations on the walls. There were paintings of kings and queens in gold frames. The ceiling of the Great Hall was decorated with murals and gargoyles. We had a banquet. King Henry VIII sat at the high table and we sat on tables along the walls. Every table was full of food! We ate pork, chicken, beef, salad, vegetables, gravy, and many other things. It was delicious! Later we were shown the library. So many bookcases filled with colourful books! There were some reading tables with open books because I think the King reads a lot. Finally we were shown the kitchen and wine cellar. The kitchen smelt of wonderful food. The cooks were very busy preparing and cooking food, not only for the banquet, but also for the 500 servants. The wine cellar was downstairs and held many barrels of wine. There was a musty smell. Thank you, King Henry, for an amazing visit!".*

Idea for the Classroom: Play: Meet Henry VIII's Wives

This play introduces Henry VIII and his six wives in turn and it also has parts for an axe-wielder and a doctor. I had some problems with the tenses in this play, but decided that Henry should speak in the present, and his wives, as ghosts, should speak in the present and past. Be creative with your costumes – robes, crowns, and the like.

Characters:

King Henry VIII
Katherine of Aragon
Anne Boleyn
Jane Seymour
Anne of Cleves
Catherine Howard
Kateryn Parr
doctor
axe-wielder

Setting:

In the gardens outside Hampton Court, the palace is in the background, to the left and right are formal trees, and there is a small fountain.

Play:

Henry: Good day. My name is King Henry VIII and I live at Hampton Court Palace. I am a generous man but I can be dangerous too.

(thunder clap)

Oh my goodness! What is that?
Katherine of Aragon: It is me, your first wife, Katherine of Aragon. I was a good wife to you for over twenty years, and I gave you a daughter, Mary. But you divorced me!
Henry: But I don't want a daughter, I want a son. Be gone!

(thunder clap)

What? Again?
Anne Boleyn: Haha! I am Anne Boleyn, Henry's second wife. We had a daughter, Elizabeth, together. But I am angry. Why? Because you had me beheaded!
Henry: Off with her head!
Axe-wielder: I will cut off your head! *(cuts off head)*.

(thunder clap)

Oh, no, not another one!
Jane Seymour: Good day, it is me, Jane Seymour. I was Henry's third wife. I gave birth to a son, Edward. But I died in childbirth.
Henry: Oh, no! Jane is dead, but now I have a son. *(thinks)* Hmmm, who shall I marry next?

(thunder clap)

Anne of Cleves: It shall be me, Anne of Cleves. I am from Germany. You must marry me.
Henry: Oh my goodness, she is so ugly! I will divorce you. Goodbye.

(thunder clap)

Catherine Howard: I am Catherine Howard, Henry's fifth wife.
Henry: Hmmm, you look nice...
Catherine Howard: I like you, Henry, but I like other men too.
Henry: Other men? But I am your husband! You are my wife! I am the King! Off with her head!
Axe-wielder: I will cut off your head! *(cuts off head)*.

(thunder clap)

Henry: Another one?

Kateryn Parr: I am Henry's last wife, Kateryn Parr. Look! Henry is so old now. I will look after him. I will be with him when he dies.
Doctor: He is very old. He is going to die soon.
Henry: Now I am very sick. It's time to die *(shrieks)* "All is lost!"

All actors take a bow

Idea for the Classroom: Ghost Concertina

Hampton Court is well known for its resident ghosts. Here's a creative way to bring some friendly ghosts into your classroom with a concertina that can be strung from wall to wall.

You need to start with a long piece of paper (cut an A4 sheet in half lengthways). Fold the paper in half lengthways and then again until you have a small square of folded paper. Draw on a ghost shape just like in the template below. Cut the shape out making sure *not* to cut down to the very bottom, or the hands. Cut a wavy line along the bottom edge. When the paper is unfolded you will have a concertina of ghosts! Cut out or draw on eyes, and stick several of these together for a spooky wall display.

GHOST CONCERTINA

cut or draw
on eyes

don't cut
the hands

don't cut to
the bottom

cut a wavy line

3.
THE
FORTH
BRIDGE

rigid cross-structure

3.
THE FORTH BRIDGE

The Forth Bridge was completed in 1890 and was an engineering marvel of its time. Even today it remains a wonder of the world and became a UNESCO World Heritage Site in 2015, and gives rise to the saying "it's like painting the Forth Bridge", referring to a seemingly never-ending task.

The red-painted bridge crosses the Firth of Forth in Scotland, connecting London and Edinburgh with Fife and Aberdeen, and serves the East Coast mainline railway. It is a cantilever bridge and has a total length of 2,467 metres (8,094 feet) and a height of 110 metres (361 feet). Construction began in 1883, and it was opened on 4th March 1890. It became a World Heritage Site in July 2015 and has become an iconic structure and symbol of Scotland.

Earlier attempts to cross the river by train started in 1850 when a 'train ferry' began, designed by Thomas Bouch. In 1878 the construction of a suspension bridge, also designed by Thomas Bouch, began. However, when Bouch's original Tay Bridge collapsed during a storm in December 1879, work on the Forth suspension bridge halted pending enquiry. Bouch's suspension bridge plans were abandoned in 1881.

New plans were made by the newly-formed Forth Bridge Railway Company. The new design had to adhere to certain specifications: the admiralty specified that the Forth remain a navigable channel, and the Board of Trade specified that the bridge must be rigid and capable of carrying the heaviest of freight trains.

In 1883 construction started with a design by John Fowler and Benjamin Baker. The bridge was completed in December 1889 and the first complete crossing took place on 24th February 1890, in which designers and dignitaries made the crossing. It was officially opened on 4th March 1990 by the Prince of Wales (later Edward VII) who drove home the last (gold-plated) rivet. This is commemorated by a plaque on the bridge.

At the time of construction it was the largest cantilever bridge in the world, and was the first all-steel bridge to be built in the UK. In total about 55,000 tonnes of steel were used. Its three double cantilevers with two 1,700 foot suspended spans are incredibly strong – at least twice as strong as it needs to be to carry the heaviest freight trains, satisfying the Board of Trade. The rail track is 46 metres (150 feet) above high water, conforming to the admiralty's specifications. 6.5 million rivets were used in its construction, and it is designed to withstand a wind force of 56lb per square foot. It was proclaimed a great milestone in the development of railway civil engineering.

Before completion, the journey from London to Aberdeen was around thirteen hours; after the bridge opened it was cut to as little as eight and a half hours, but was generally around ten hours. These days around 200 trains cross the bridge each day, both local and high-speed. Around three million passengers cross the bridge each year.

The expression "It's like painting the Forth Bridge" popularly means a never-ending or tedious task, and refers to the fact that as soon as the bridge had been painted from end to end, the painters had to start from the other end again. Network Rail reported in 2001 that a ten year programme of repainting and refurbishment would begin in 2002, thus painting the structure fully for the first time in its history. In the process, all previous layers of paint were removed and three new coats applied totalling 240,000 litres of paint. 1,500 people were involved in the project, with up to 400 people working on the bridge each day. Apparently the new coat will last for twenty years, putting an end (at least temporarily) to the myth that painting the Forth Bridge is a never-ending task.

In 2012 the Department of Culture, Media and Sport announced a nomination would be prepared to enlist the bridge as a UNESCO World Heritage Site. Over the next three years came a lengthy public consultation over the nomination, followed by a submission. The application was successful, and on 5th July 2015 the Forth Bridge was formally named a UNESCO World Heritage Site. It is the sixth World Heritage Site in Scotland.

This coincided with the 125th anniversary of the completion of the bridge. A number of special events were held throughout 2015 to celebrate, the highlight of which was the Forth Bridges Festival in September, celebrating all three bridges (one rail and two road) across the Firth of Forth.

The Forth Bridge is a railway bridge, so it would seem obvious to visit the area by train. There are services from Edinburgh Waverly station that take about twenty minutes to Dalmeny (on the south side) or North Queensferry (on the north side). Also, don't forget to actually cross the bridge by train!

Other than by train, you can access the bridge area by car from the A90, which crosses the Forth Road Bridge, or by bus with service number 43 from Edinburgh Bus Station to Dalmeny on the south side or North Queensferry on the north side. You might like to splash out on a 'Forth Bridges Bus and Boat Tour' that takes in all the main sites, and starts from Edinburgh city centre (see goscotlandtours.com, for example).

Once you are there, there are a number of viewpoints, footpaths and trails. There is also a Contact and Education Centre in its own purpose-built facility on the south side. Its aim is "to provide high-quality contact, outreach and education services to local residents and visitors". In particular there is a schools programme, allowing children to find out about science, technology and engineering, and also about the site itself.

It is well worth a visit if you are in the Edinburgh area; it is an iconic symbol of both Scotland and engineering achievement, and "remains a potent symbol of Britain's industrial, scientific, architectural and transport heritage".

Idea for the Classroom: Design your own set of coins

In 2004 the Forth Bridge was commemorated on the £1 coin. The depiction on the coin shows the magnificent cantilevers of the bridge and was designed by the wood engraver Edwina Ellis. The border around the outside of the coin is a railway track. There is no inscription on the edge of the coin, just a zig-zag pattern which draws inspiration from the shape of the bridge. In common with all £1 coins the diameter is 22.5mm, weight 9.5g, thickness 3.15mm, and composition nickel-brass (70% copper, 5.5% nickel and 24.5% zinc). In total almost forty million were minted.

Here's your chance to design your own set of three coins based on an important landmark, person or event. First choose your theme: think of famous or historic buildings in your area; think of famous people who inspire you or from TV; think of important events that have happened recently. Each coin can have one different place, person or event, with the most important being on the highest denomination. Don't forget to specify the value of the coins, how big they are, and what they are made of.

Idea for the Classroom: Cardboard Bridge

Why not make a bridge of your own out of old cardboard boxes? You need a load of old cardboard (for example like they use to pack fridges and TVs in) and check that it is safe as there are often large sharp staples that were used to hold the box together.

Design your bridge! The most basic design is to have two towers, one at either end, with a roadway suspended between, following in the style of Tower Bridge in London. These suspension bridges have a lot of give – in other words they can move and sway in the wind. The second of our bridges is the cantilever bridge with a strong cross-cross of struts for support, as with the Forth Bridge. Cantilever bridges are very rigid and very strong, so that even the heaviest goods trains can pass over them. A final way is to design a bridge with arches made from card, with a roadway on top – a very strong form of bridge that is common in Roman architecture. It is a useful form of bridge for shallow rivers, and a similar style has been used with many of London's bridges.

Look at the diagrams for these three types of design (below). Which is the strongest? Try making your bridge from cardboard, string, or toy building blocks. You can decorate your bridge, give it doors and windows or even buildings. And, of course, don't forget to paint your bridge!

Idea for the Classroom: World Heritage Sites of Scotland

There are 29 UNESCO World Heritage Sites in the UK, and the Forth Bridge is the sixth UNESCO World Heritage Site in Scotland. But what are the other five? They are:

1. The Frontiers of the Roman Empire (the Antonine Wall)
2. St. Kilda
3. Edinburgh Old and New Towns
4. New Lanark
5. The Heart of Neolithic Orkney

Choose one of the other World Heritage Sites (or one of the 29 in the UK if you prefer) and find out about it. Try to find out:

- What is the site? An island, town, monument?
- Where is it in Scotland?
- When was it made a World Heritage Site?
- How can you travel there?
- What is your opinion of the site?
- Any other information?

Try making a poster for your site, with a picture. Use the information you found out before on your poster, and then present them to your classmates. Below I have made a Forth Bridges Festival poster as an example. I tried to choose a border that looks like the Forth Bridge, and included some of the information for visitors.

Forth Bridge Pound Coin

Value: £1
Made of: nickel-brass
Diameter: 22.5mm
Thickness: 3.15mm
Weight: 9.5g
Number minted: 40 million
Mint date: 2004

Design Your Own Coins

Value:
Made of:
Diameter:
Thickness:
Weight:
Number minted:
Mint date:

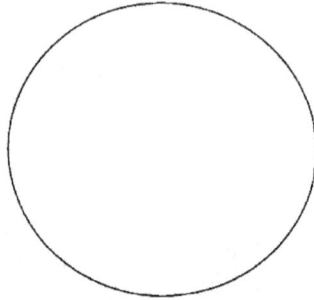

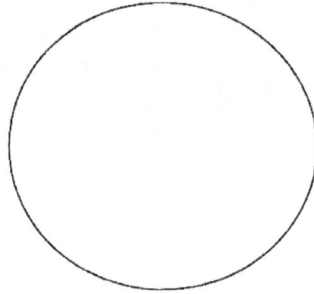

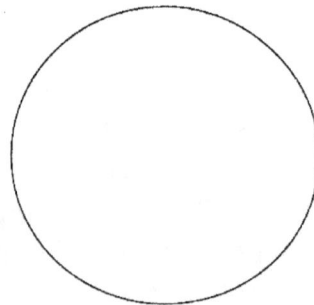

Value:
Made of:
Diameter:
Thickness:
Weight:
Number minted:
Mint date:

Value:
Made of:
Diameter:
Thickness:
Weight:
Number minted:
Mint date:

Three Types of Bridge

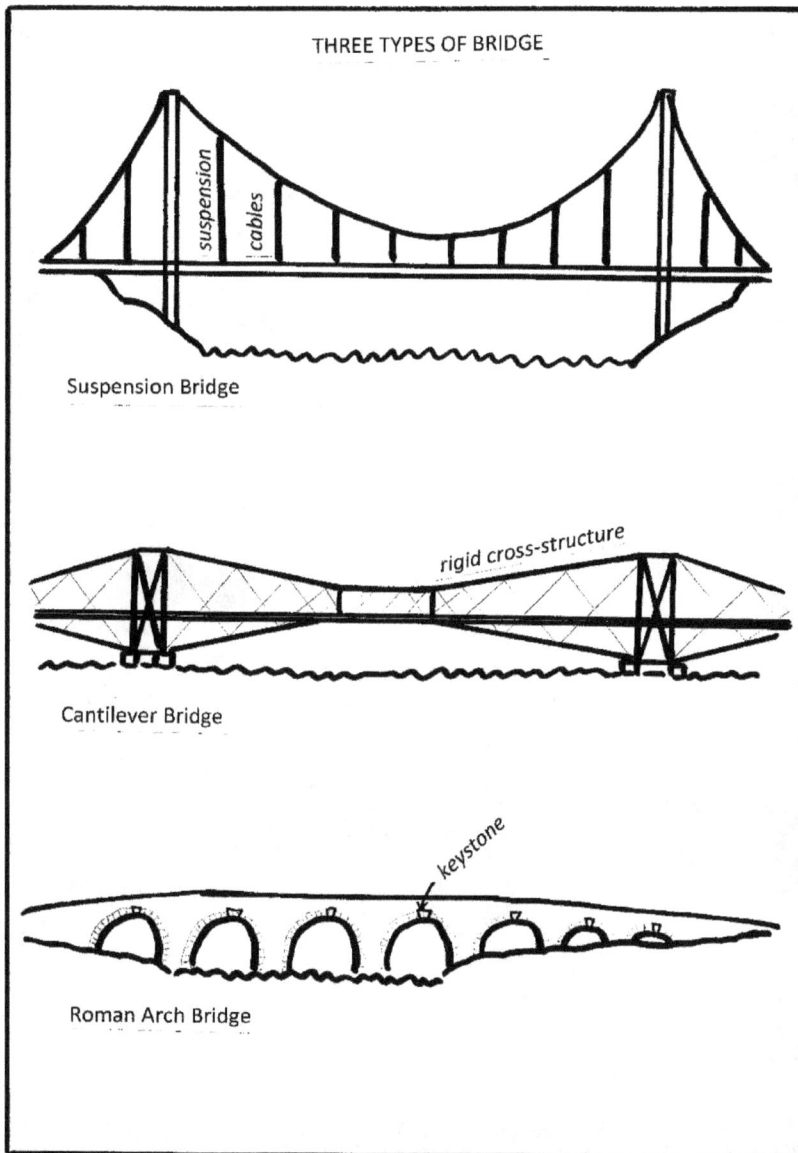

Suspension Bridge

Cantilever Bridge

Roman Arch Bridge

Forth Bridges Festival 2015

4.
THE
LONDON
UNDERGROUND

FARRINGDON

4.

THE LONDON UNDERGROUND

The world's first underground railway celebrated its 150th anniversary in 2013 and its bulls-eye motif and stylised map design have become iconic symbols of London.

The idea of an underground railway was first put forward by Charles Pearson in the 1830s as a solution to London's busy and overcrowded streets, but at first the idea was ridiculed. In 1846 a parliamentary commission was established to survey the state of London's transport, and it concluded that an underground railway was the best option. In 1853/4 the Commons passed a bill approving the construction of Pearson's Metropolitan District Railway and in 1860 construction started using the 'cut and cover' method. It ran from Paddington through the Fleet Valley and reached the city at Farringdon.

On 9th January 1863 the Metropolitan Railway was finally unveiled, with the opening ceremony held at Paddington. Dignitaries were driven the six kilometres to Farringdon. On the following day the line was open to the public and became a popular attraction. In those days there were three classes of carriage; these early trains had no windows because there was seen to be no need for them. The seats were high-backed and quilted and so came to be known as padded cells.

But there were some major problems. The steam locomotives produced lots of smoke and smell, and ventilating the tunnels was a problem, and the tunnels themselves became dirty very quickly. Along the route of the railway over one thousand houses were demolished and 12,000 people were displaced, often the poorest who lived in slums. Nonetheless the success of the Metropolitan Railway encouraged other projects, and soon London was abuzz with underground fever.

In 1890 the Stockwell line was the first to be electrified and many of the problems of smoke and dirt disappeared. Unlike the Metropolitan Railway, it charged the same rate for any journey (2d – two old pence) and all the carriages were of identical class. Other lines followed suit with electrification, for example the Circle line in 1905. The idea of trains running through tubes was established, and the system soon became known as 'the tube'.

By 1908 it was clear that the various underground railway companies had to work together to create a unified system, so the managers of the various companies met to try and decide a common name for the system. Various names were put forward including the 'Tube' or the 'Electric', but finally the name 'Underground' was chosen. Two other results of the meetings was that each line was assigned a colour, and the bullseye motif was adopted.

The Underground continued to grow haphazardly and without much logical planning. Some kind of logical order needed to be imposed and it came in the form of Harry Beck's underground map.

Born in Leyton in 1903, in his twenties he worked as an engineering draughtsman at the London Underground Signals

Office. In 1931 he proposed a radical new design based on electrical circuit diagrams. Beck could see that the system had become too big to be represented geographically, and that a schematic representation based on horizontals, verticals and diagonals would be better. Beck himself said he wanted to 'tidy up' the map "by straightening the lines, experimenting with diagonals and evening out the distance between stations".

Streets were removed from the map, and only a stylised line for the Thames remained. Diamonds (and later circles) represented interchange stations. The lines in the City of London were expanded to give a clearer diagrammatic representation; similarly the outlying lines were compressed and the gaps between stations evened out. Stations that were not interchanges were shown as 'ticks' (short lines at right angles to the lines). The total effect is to give the illusion of logic to what is in effect a haphazard and chaotic system: a utopian view of London.

Though Beck's design was not approved when he first submitted it in 1931, it was eventually accepted in 1933 and was printed as pocket maps and wall posters. Beck's map became instantly popular with the public, and it is still used as the basis of the Underground's maps today.

To great fanfare 2013 marked the 150th anniversary of the London Underground. As BBC news reported, on 10th January a steam train recreated the journey of the first underground train – from Paddington to Farringdon. The BBC reports that although the original line only comprised seven stops, it was an instant hit attracting up to 40,000 people on its first day back in 1863.

The guardian.com (9th January 2013) offered a useful timeline as part of its series on the 150th anniversary. Some notable dates adapted from the Guardian's 'condensed history' are:

- *1863 the world's first underground train line, the Metropolitan Railway, opens from Paddington to Farringdon Street;*
- *1868 District line between Westminster and South Kensington opens on Christmas Eve;*
- *1884 Circle Line opens, connecting Metropolitan and District Lines;*
- *1900 Central Line opens;*
- *1905 District and Circle Lines are electrified;*
- *1911 first escalator on the system opened at Earl's Court;*
- *1924 Northern Line opens;*
- *1933 Harry Beck unveils his diagrammatic map;*
- *1940 Underground used as air raid shelters during Second World War;*
- *1968 Victoria Line opens;*
- *1979 Jubilee Line opens;*
- *2003 Oyster travel cards introduced;*
- *2007 London Underground reaches 1 million passengers a year;*
- *2013 150th Anniversary;*
- *2015 plans unveiled to extend the Northern Line to Battersea.*

It is interesting that many of the deep level stations are higher than the tracks: this assists deceleration when arriving and acceleration when departing. There are four rails that make up the track, namely two running rails and two live rails, and make up a four-rail DC system.

But the tube is not just a practical and mechanical transport system; it is also a living, breathing thing akin to a living creature. Ackroyd points to this living, human dimension, writing in his book that every line has its own identity and mood, even according to time of day. He notes the Northern line is 'intense and moody', the Central Line has 'purpose and energy', the Circle Line is 'adventurous and breezy', whilst the Bakerloo is 'disconsolate and brooding'. The Underground's atmosphere also varies according to time of day: in the afternoon it becomes sleepy and even luxuriant; during the rush hour it is crowded, noisy and maddening; by late evening it becomes more dark and sinister, a "haven for the drunk".

"Getting there" describes itself, as the tube extends to many far-flung suburban corners of London so it is always nearby. So, take a train to whatever part interests you. For me the most interesting lines are the deep lines, where the passenger descends by long escalators into a subterranean world of signs, maps and passageways. Take the Northern, Bakerloo or Victoria lines, for example, with northbound trains one way, southbound the other. The lines have a musty (but well ventilated) odour, as the carriages clatter over the tracks into the station. During rush hour, at busy stations, you can hear the classic 'MIND THE GAP' announcement.

I would suggest taking the tube to Covent Garden to see the London Transport Museum (www.ltmuseum.co.uk) that houses a fine collection of trams, buses and early tube trains. Of interest to us is an original steam engine from the Metropolitan Railway dating from 1866, in use until 1905 when the line was electrified. There is also a 'padded cell' passenger carriage used on the City & South London Railway from 1890 to 1924. The carriage formed part of the first deep level tube trains, and featured a conductor who announced the station names for the passengers. There are special exhibitions in addition to the permanent collection, for example 'London Moving' and 'Poster Art' events scheduled for 2016. The museum is open every day from 10am to 6pm, and your ticket gives you unlimited admission for six months.

For information on the system go to https://tfl.gov.uk, or one of the many tourist information sites on places to visit in the capital. Or why not take the Circle Line from Paddington to Farringdon to recreate the original railway? And remember – the journey is just as important as the destination. *Stand clear of the doors, please!*

Idea for the Classroom: The Underground Facts & Figures

There are eleven lines on the London Underground, each signified by a different colour. You will need to look at the Wikipedia page *https://en.wikipedia.org/wiki/London_Underground* to fill out this chart, then answer the questions below. The first part of the chart has been done for you. Find the completed chart in two pages' time!

London Underground Lines

Line	Colour	Opened	Type	Length	Stations
Bakerloo	brown	1906	deep tube	23.2km 14.5m	25
Central					
Circle					
District					
Hammersmith & City					
Jubilee					
Metropolitan					
Northern					
Piccadilly					
Victoria					
Waterloo & City					

Questions

a. How many lines are there?
b. What lines are coloured red, green and light blue?
c. What lines are coloured pink, purple and turquoise?
d. What was the first line to open?
e. What line was opened most recently?
f. How many of the lines are sub surface?
g. How many of the lines are deep tube?
h. What is the longest line?
i. What is the shortest line?
j. What line has the most stations?
k. What is the total number of stations?
l. What is the total length of all the lines put together? (You may need a calculator!).

Answers: a. 11 b. Central, District, Victoria c. Hammersmith & City, Metropolitan, Waterloo & City d. Metropolitan e. Jubilee f. 4 g. 7 h. Central i. Waterloo & City j. District k. 381 l. 469.3km / 292.5m.

Idea for the Classroom: Make your own Station Sign

The 'bulls-eye' design is an iconic symbol not only of the Underground but also of London. The circle is a red colour and the stripe containing the name is blue with lettering in white. Now's your chance to design your own bulls-eye: you can either follow the same design and colouring as the original or come up with something completely different. I have made a template of the original bulls-eye below if you want to use it, plus a few ideas for alternative templates. Decorate them according to your own choice, and choose the station name that you want. These signs can look very effective on a wall display and tie in well to a class project on transport, place names, or the history of London.

Idea for the Classroom: 150th Anniversary Poster

In 2013 the London Underground celebrated its 150th year anniversary. To help in the celebration it's time to design a poster that would be suitable for display on the Underground walls. Your poster should include: a title, a party or celebration to which the public is invited, a date and time for the event, a location, and any other special information about the event (What can visitors see and do? Is food and drink available? Is there an admission fee?). Look at my example below for a 100th anniversary; your poster should be colourful and eye-catching!

London Underground Lines: Completed Chart

Line	Colour	Opened	Type	Length	Stations
Bakerloo	brown	1906	deep tube	23.2km 14.5m	25
Central	red	1900	deep tube	74km 46m	49
Circle	yellow	1871	sub surface	27.2km 17m	36
District	green	1868	sub surface	64km 40m	60
Hammersmith & City	pink	1864	sub surface	25.5km 15.9m	29
Jubilee	grey	1979	deep tube	36.2km 22.5m	27
Metropolitan	purple	1863	sub surface	66.7km 41.5m	34
Northern	black	1890	deep tube	58km 36m	50
Piccadilly	dark blue	1906	deep tube	71km 44.3m	53
Victoria	light blue	1968	deep tube	21km 13.3m	16
Waterloo & City	turquoise	1898	deep tube	2.5km 1.5m	2

'Bullseye' Template

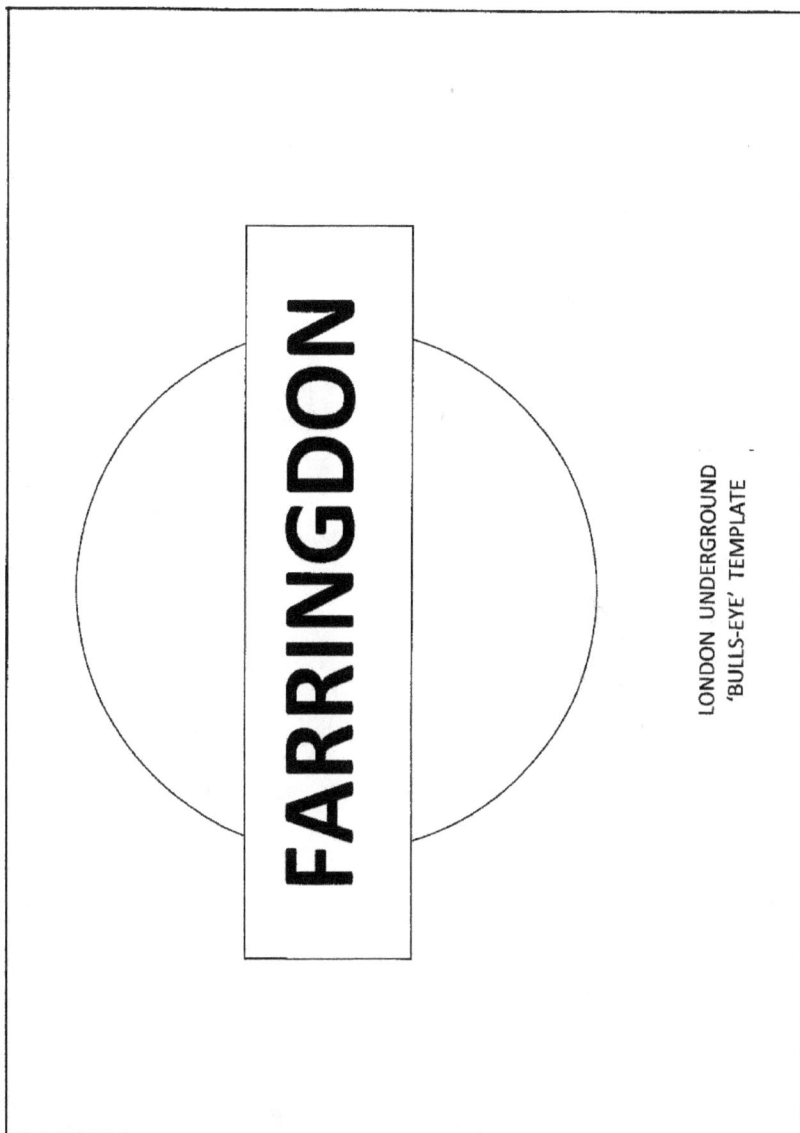

FARRINGDON

LONDON UNDERGROUND
'BULLS-EYE' TEMPLATE

Station Sign Ideas

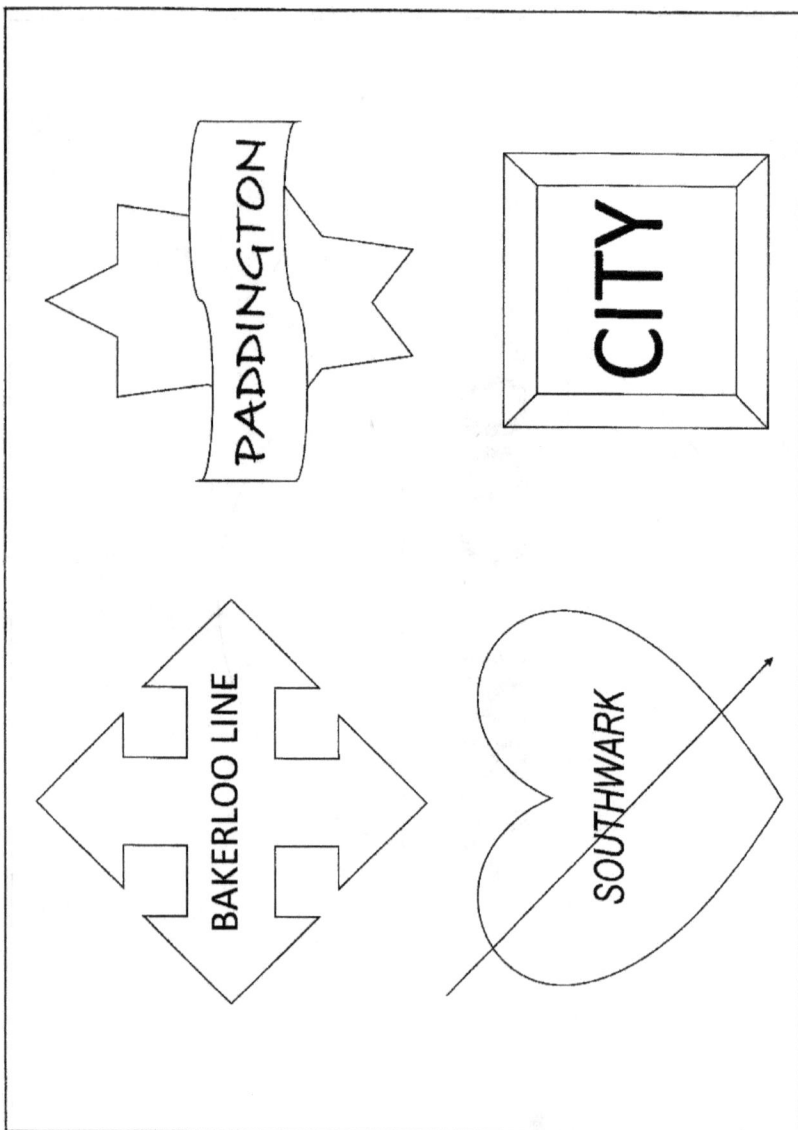

Anniversary Poster Example

BARRY'S UNDERGROUND RAILWAY

100th Anniversary

Tuesday 27th October 2015

CITY OF LONDON

Display of antique trains
Ride on the first steam train
Eat and drink for free!

Admission adults: £7.50 children: free!

5.
THE WELSH
SHOW CAVES

5.
THE WELSH
SHOW CAVES

If you fancy a different kind of life underground... and you happen to be in the Brecon Beacons National Park in South Wales... then how about a visit to the Dan Yr Ogof showcave and its surrounding attractions? Many carboniferous limestone caves 'lurk' beneath the National Park, and a great deal of them are inaccessible apart from those around Dan Yr Ogof, located in the Upper Swansea Valley.

The National Showcaves Centre for Wales is a proud collection of attractions, not only the caves themselves but also the Shire Horse Centre, Millenium Stone Circle, and life-size dinosaur models.

The River Llynfell travels underground for 6 km before it emerges at Dan Yr Ogof Cave, and of course it is the extensive cave system that is the main attraction. It comprises a stunning underground world of stalactites and chambers, and is one of the largest networks of subterranean passageways in Britain. Formation of the limestone caves started 315 million years ago, and over time the cracks and fissures in the rock has allowed the flow of water dissolving the stone and carving out the system we see today.

Back in 1912 two brothers, Tommy and Jeff Morgan discovered the caves and started to explore them using only very basic equipment like candles to light the way and rope for the few dangerous climbs within. Their way into the caves was by coracle (a small circular canoe with paddles) over the small lake that is now known as Coracle Pool. They plotted their route through the caves by marking the sand and mud with arrows. When the brothers reached the Bridge Chamber they discovered a further two lakes. They discovered interesting formations at this time such as the 'Rasher of Bacon' and the heavenly 'Angel'.

And so ended the first chapter in the caves' exploration until the 1930s and, together with further exploration in the 1960s, a further 10 miles of passageways was revealed. In 1963 Eileen Davies made further exploration that led to the discovery of over 16 km of passageways.

Let's take a look at some of the caves and caverns that were found, and what today's visitor can see in each.

First and foremost is the Dan Yr Ogof Cave, famous not only for its stalactites and stalacmites, but also for its rare helectites which grow out sideways, and its limestone 'curtains'. I find the entrance interesting: whereas the Morgan Brothers had to crawl through an opening barely wide enough, the modern-day visitor is treated to a generous man-made tunnel. Once inside we are able to wander along about a kilometre of well-paved passageways, though unfortunately the many steps and steep gradients in places make a visit by the disabled impossible.

Nearby is the Cathedral Cave, a small tunnel-like cave, discovered in 1953 by members of the South Wales Caving Club. Though at first the entrance was a bit of a squeeze through a narrow passageway, they were able to use controlled explosives to blast out a bigger entrance to allow better access to the cave. What they found was a passageway decorated with thousands of delicate 'straw' stalactites. Located at 150 metres below the surface, the Cathedral Cave is in places 10 metres high. The most impressive formation is a large 40 foot waterfall, known as the Dome of St Paul, that visitors can walk behind. The combination of subterranean waterfalls and lakes is truly amazing.

Stroll up to the Bone Cave for more of interest. Here, 42 human skeletons dating back to the Bronze Age (3,000 years ago) were found. Other items found here include silver rings, fragments of Roman pottery, coins, and bronze jewelry. There is an exhibit here showing man's use of caves in the past, and some other living things that have lived hereabouts – including hyenas, wolves and bears. In fact the oldest bone in the cave is that of a red dear at over 7,000 years old.

Also in the Bone Cave look out for unusual stalactites in the form of huge bosses (circular domes) covered in a white deposit resembling yoghurt. Because of its texture it has been given the nickname 'Moonmilk', and is in essence a kind of white mud.

In the three caves are exhibits of various scenes of cave life. One depicts an ancient burial ceremony; another shows a Bronze Age family carrying out typical daily tasks; and one further exhibit shows archaeologists at work, using survey instruments, photographic equipment, sieves and grids. One interesting display is of cave paintings, their subject and meaning. Though only in the colours of brown, red, yellow and black, they offer a glimpse into life in the Bronze Age.

For those interested in prehistoric animals there are over 200 life-size models of dinosaurs, ranged around the site, both inside and outside the caves. Apparently it is one of the world's largest dinosaur parks and has in itself won awards. The official website encourages us to "get up close and personal" with the monsters, including a Tyrannosaurus Rex. I'm not sure, personally, whether I'd like to get up close and personal with a T-Rex, even if it is made of plastic and fibre-glass. Of more interest to me is the website which has a lot of resources for children including a colouring competition, a memory test game, and a quiz: can you name the dinosaurs? Match a name to a dinosaur outline and "submit" your answer!

There's a few other attractions of note like the Millenium Stone Circle, Shire Horse Centre, Fossil House, Iron Age Farm, caravan & tent site, coffee shop, gift and shop. In all ten attractions are included in the entry ticket, which at the time of publishing was £7.80 for adults and £4.80 for children. Visiting is self-guided, with audio commentaries which, though a little outdated, give a good sense of atmosphere. Some of the music playing is, however, a bit overdone and at times I was left wondering if contemplating the stones and stalactites in silence might not be a better option. Those with deeper pockets and sufficient inclination can opt for the Ski Centre and Trekking Centre, and the Cathedral Cave is even licensed for underground weddings!

Reviews suggest that it is well worth the visit and our old friend *Tripadvisor* uses phrases such as "a great family day out", "awesome", "amazing" and "wow" in typical review style. It looks as if the caves' manager is on the ball too, as he ("Dan O") replies to most reviews. *Dayoutwiththekids.co.uk* similarly writes of a "must see attraction... magical" and a "thoroughly enjoyable day". The best of these reviews (all taken from 2015) and slightly unbelievable is the comment "breathtaking 10/10 AAA+++ 5 Star".

For those more inclined to serious caving, contact can be made with the South Wales Caving Club which runs expeditions from advanced level all the way down to absolute beginners on their 'Try Caving Weekends'. All visitors are guided by a warden and must have or hire suitable clothing and equipment. This kind of activity is not up my street, and I prefer the virtual tour the club provides of the caves on the internet.

Getting there is easy by private car or public bus. The easiest way is from the M4 to the south: leave at junction 45 and follow the signs for the A4067 North. You will see the brown tourist signs for the Dan Yr Ogof Caves which you can follow all the way up the valley. It should take about twenty minutes. From Brecon to the north access is via the A40 and A4067. Onsite parking is free. There is a regular public bus service all year – see the Traveline Cymru public transport information service online for details. Opening hours are 10am to 3pm (3:30 during Welsh school holidays).

It seems there are a lot more caverns and formations to be found in the area, too. As the website puts it: "Who knows what might be discovered tomorrow?".

Idea for the Classroom: Cave Painting

The earliest examples of cave paintings in Europe have been found in the Chauvet Cave in France, Coliboaia Cave in Romania, and El Castillo Cave in Spain. They depict figurative humans and animals and are believed to be around 35,000 years old. In ancient times cavemen used resin, dyes charcoal and animal bones to make colours. However, only a limited number of colours could be produced – red, brown, yellow and black – giving the paintings their characteristic colour style.

The surface of cave walls is rough and not ideal for painting. Replicate this surface with rough cardboard or try tearing a piece of cardboard in two lengthways (the difficult way), or prepare thick paper or card by painting on a coat of sand mixed with glue.

Then the fun starts! Choose your theme: animals, warriors, trees or rocks are good starting points. Below I have given a couple of templates: one for a bull, one for a group of warriors. Imagine a caveman hunting the bull with spears and arrows!

Idea for the Classroom: Fossils and Rubbings

Another way of exploring texture and how it effects artwork is to make rubbings – ideally of fossils, but other items work well too – tree bark, leaves, coins, stony ground, or cloth material, for example.

You might already have a collection of fossils at school or your local museum may have one or two you could borrow. Tree bark comes in a variety of textures – the fine texture of pine bark or the rough texture of an oak. While you're out in the playground find some leaves and try these too. Have a go at taking a rubbing from a stony path and compare it to the result you get from concrete or plaster. If you are careful, make a rubbing of a computer keyboard (switch it off first!) or find some street signs or number plates on cars.

Idea for the Classroom: Dinosaur Matching Game

Match the dinosaur to its description. Description words can include the following:

body
fat body
thin body
wings
spikes

head / face
long nose
big eyes
horns
large mouth
teeth

neck and tail
long neck
short neck
long tail
short tail
strong tail
pointed tail

legs
two legs
four legs
short front legs
long back legs

standing position
on all fours
upright
on its rear legs

Once the students are familiar with these words you can try matching the descriptions with the pictures below. Note that the descriptions below match the names and pictures space-by-space. You can try a describe and draw activity too!

Cave Paintings – Bull

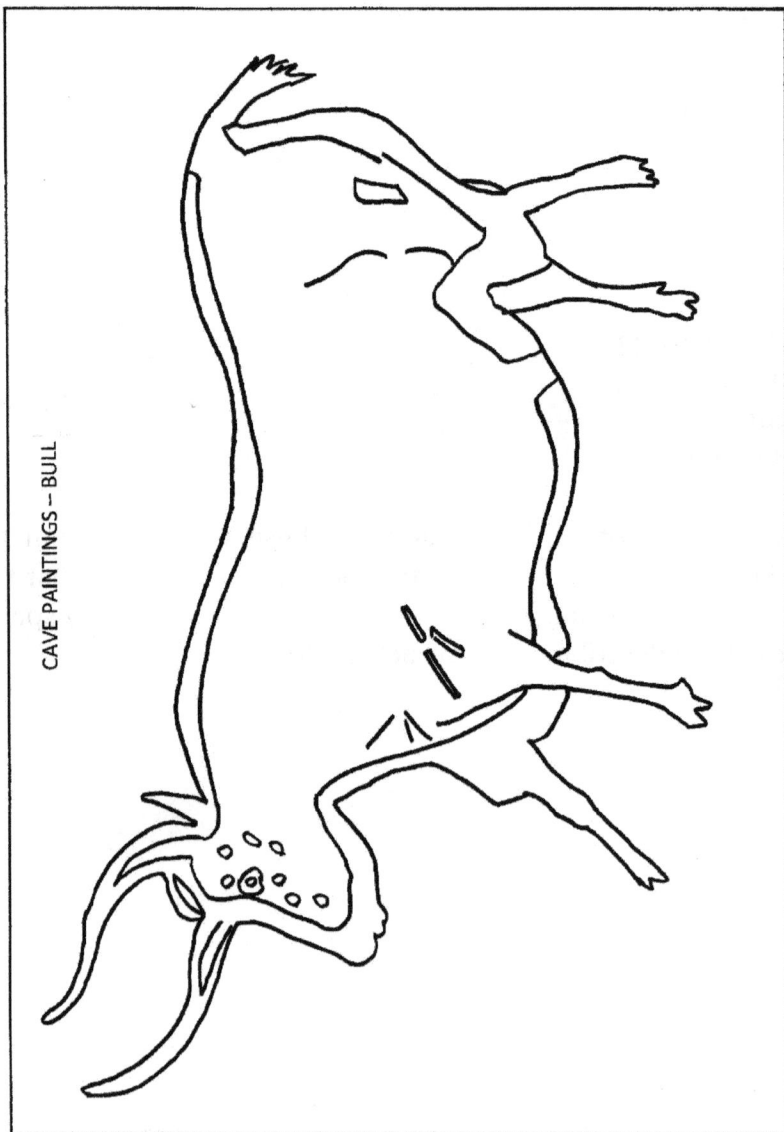

CAVE PAINTINGS – BULL

Cave Paintings – Warriors

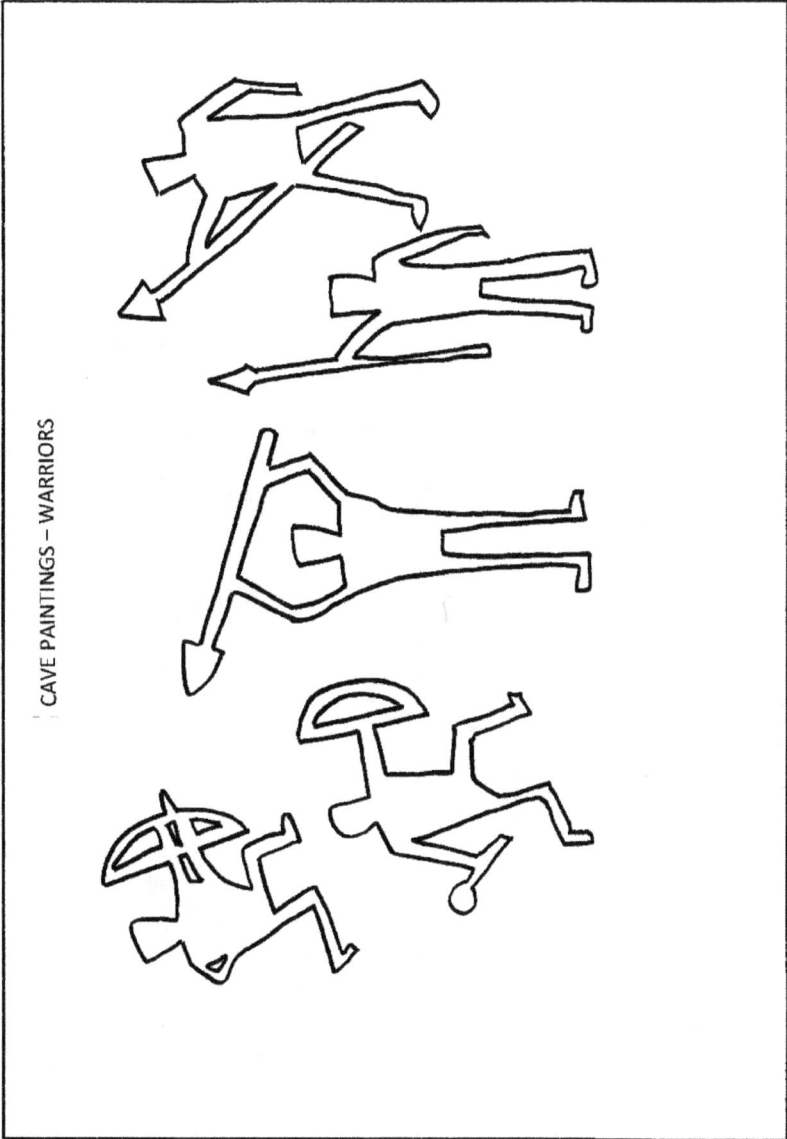

CAVE PAINTINGS – WARRIORS

Fossils and Other Rubbings

fossil #1

fossil #2

tree bark

street sign

computer keys

Dinosaur Matching: Descriptions

This dinosaur has a fat body, four legs, and stands on all fours. It has a cute happy face with big eyes and a long nose. It has spikes along its back.	This is a flying dinosaur with a long body and long wings. It has big eyes and two horns. It has two legs. Its tail is long with a point at the end.
This is a large dinosaur with two short front legs and two long back legs. It is standing upright. Its face is fat with big eyes. It has a strong powerful tail.	This dinosaur is fat and has four legs. It has no neck. Above its face are two horns and on its short nose is another horn. Its tail is wide and short.
This dinosaur has a fat body, but a long neck and a long tail. Its face is small with cute eyes and a big mouth. It has four short legs.	This dinosaur has a fat body, a large head, and no neck. It has two horns on the sides of its head. It has four legs and feet with claws. Its tail is short and strong.

Dinosaur Matching: Pictures

stegosaurus 	**pterosaur** 
tyrannosaurus 	**triceratops** 
brachiosaurus 	**protoceratops** 

6.
THE MURDER
OF
THOMAS BECKET

6.
THE MURDER OF
THOMAS BECKET

The murder of Thomas Becket remains one of the most important events of Medieval England, and shows how two friends can become enemies with catastrophic results.

Thomas Becket was born on 21st December 1118 in Cheapside, London. At the age of ten he was sent to Merton Priory School, Sussex, and later a grammar school in London and finally a university in Paris. With his parents' death he worked as a clerk in the household of Theobald of Bec who was then Archbishop of Canterbury.

By then his personality was starting to show: a strongly-built, spirited youth, a lover of field sports, hawking and hunting. He also loved conversation and was frank and straightforward in speech. He had good administrative skills, charm, intelligence and diplomacy.

Theobald recommended him to Henry II for the post of Lord Chancellor (chief minister) and he duly took up the post in January 1155. As Lord Chancellor he enforced the king's sources of revenue and helped set up many matters of state. They were also good friends, having similar personalities and interests: hunting, playing jokes and socialising. It was in many respects a luxurious 'high life'.

Henry II thought that it would be good to have a trusted friend in the position of Archbishop of Canterbury, and tried to persuade Becket to take the post when it became vacant. Knowing of the king's fearsome temper, at first he refused, saying "our friendship will turn to hate". Finally he relented and accepted the position on 3rd June 1162. Henry's idea was that by having his friend as Archbishop he could easily impose his will upon the Church – but he was mistaken.

Becket underwent a change of character as Archbishop, and his allegiance shifted from the royal court to the Church and he started to take a stand against the king. He stopped his luxurious lifestyle, ate bread and drank water, slept on the floor, and wore a horse hair shirt under his fine robes. He spent much time with charity, distribution of food to the poor, visiting the infirmary, reading and discussing scriptures and supervising monks at their work.

What this meant in practice was that he was increasingly at odds with Henry II. This was particularly so with the issue of the courts. There were two courts in England: the Crown (Royal) Court and the Church Court. Any member of the Church who was accused of a crime could opt to be tried in a Church Court rather than a Crown Court. Church Courts usually gave easier punishments, for example a thief was sent on a pilgrimage.

Henry II increasingly felt that Becket's actions undermined his authority, and that England was becoming too lawless – the Church didn't set a good example as its courts were too lenient on offenders. Things came to a head with the trial of Canon Philip de Brois (1163) who was accused of murdering a soldier. He was tried in a church court and acquitted, and only ordered to pay a fine to the deceased man's family. The crown court then stepped in and attempted to try him; Henry changed the law to extend the crown court's jurisdiction. His 1164 law stated that any person found guilty in a church court could be punished by a crown court. Becket refused to agree to this.

The rift increased, until eventually Becket fled to France for fear of his life, and remained in exile for six years.

After this time in exile there was a reconciliation in 1170, but this did not last long as Becket suffered at the hands of Henry's bad temper. Becket had threatened to excommunicate his opponents, including the Archbishop of York, because of their support for the king during his exile. This pushed Henry II over the top, as he declared "who will rid me of this troublesome priest?".

Four of his knights took this seriously as a royal command, and set out to Canterbury to confront Becket. An atmosphere of foreboding hung over Canterbury, and Becket even received a letter warning him of danger. On 29th December 1170 the knights arrived in Canterbury. At first they met with Becket and tried to reason with him, but Becket would not give in. Upon this, the four knights wielded their swords and caught up with him near the stairs to the crypt, just as the monks were chanting vespers in the quire.

They struck him three times with their swords, and at the third blow Becket fell to his knees proclaiming "For the name of Jesus and the protection of the Church, I am ready to embrace death". The final blow was fatal, and the knights fled with the words "Let us away, knights; this fellow will arise no more".

Becket's body lay in the middle of the transept, and for a time no one dared approach. A thunderstorm was looming overhead.

The effects of the murder were felt all over Europe, and most laid the blame firmly with his former friend, Henry II.

When Henry heard of the murder he was full of remorse, and shut himself in his rooms and fasted for forty days. The king later performed public penance: he wore a sack-cloth and walked barefoot through the streets of Canterbury whilst monks flogged him with branches. He then spent the night in the Cathedral's crypt.

On 21st February 1173 Becket was canonised and made a saint. The number of pilgrims visiting Canterbury grew rapidly and his tomb became a shrine and was relocated to the newly-built Trinity Chapel. The shrine was magnificently decorated with gold, silver and jewels, and people left valuables there in respect. Several miracles were said to occur at the tomb, and a visit there was claimed to free people of illness and disease.

The shrine survived until 1538 when it was destroyed during the Dissolution of the Monasteries on the orders of Henry VIII. Today, the site of the shrine is marked with a single lit candle.

"When his time of testing came, he had the courage to lay down his life to defend the ancient rights of the Church against the aggressive state".

Thomas Becket has left us a fine legacy. If you go to Canterbury you can see for yourself the magnificent cathedral that was built on the proceeds of gifts and the sale of official souvenirs over the few centuries that followed. The cathedral inspired Geoffrey Chaucer's *The Canterbury Tales* in which pilgrims make their way from Southwark in London to Becket's shrine. We can see the magnificent Miracle Window, showing in colourful stained glass the story of Thomas Becket and the miracles attributed to him. The feast of St. Thomas of Canterbury is now celebrated throughout the Roman Catholic Church, and in England he is regarded as the protector of the secular clergy.

Visitors and pilgrims to Canterbury today have a lot to see. The city itself has a well-preserved medieval centre, with narrow streets and timber-framed buildings. It is not too difficult to imagine the king dressed in sack-cloth walking the streets in penance. Don't forget the Westgate Museum, housed within the West Gate on the city walls, with perhaps the best views over Canterbury from the battlements. Children will enjoy the Canterbury Tales exhibition, showing life in the medieval city from the comfort of a mini-train.

In the cathedral itself the place where Thomas Becket was murdered is marked with a memorial depicting the four swords that led to his end (two swords made of metal, two more the shadows of these swords). Where the shrine once stood, a single candle burns with a glowing light.

Getting to Canterbury is easy from London, and a day-trip is possible. The fastest route is from St. Pancras station on the Javelin train which follows the Eurostar route for much of its course. After passing Ashford, the train slows and ambles through a green valley of oast houses and apple orchards. There are trains every half hour from St. Pancras, and the journey takes just under an hour.

By car follow the M2 and then turn off onto the A2 at Faversham to Canterbury. From the M20 turn off onto the A249 that will bring you on to the M2 as above. Parking might be a problem as the centre of the city is pedestrianised; park in an outlying area and take a bus or walk into the centre.

There is no shortage of restaurants, pubs and shops in Canterbury. The Weavers Cottage restaurant, the Sun Inn, or

Nasons Department Store spring to mind. Maps and guidebooks are widely available.

Idea for the Classroom: Stained Glass Window

Look at the black and white window of Saint Thomas Becket at Canterbury Cathedral I have drawn below. Just imagine this window in beautiful stained glass! There are two ways to do this: the easiest way is simply to colour the picture! But the best way is to make a real 'stained glass' window using tissue paper – stick with it and the result is very satisfying. All you need is some colourful tissue paper, perhaps odds and ends left over from the last project. Then, carefully, use a sharp knife to cut out some of the shapes in the template – I'd recommend just cutting the main features such as the facial features, hands, parts of the robe, the Bible and, of course the 'halo' of light around Becket's head. Stick the tissue paper over the spaces you've cut out, on one side only. When finished, turn it over and the colours should show neatly. When dry, stick your art on a window so that the light can shine through it.

Idea for the Classroom: Canterbury Train Timetable

Planning a trip to Canterbury? Take a look at the extract below (based on the timetable of summer 2015) and answer the questions:

1. What time does the fastest train from St. Pancras to Canterbury West depart?
2. What time does the fastest train from Canterbury West to St. Pancras depart?
3. I want to go to St. Pancras in the evening. Which train shouldn't I take?

4. I want to be in Canterbury by midday. Which train should I take?
5. Which train departs from Canterbury East?
6. How long does the 17:37 train from Canterbury West to St. Pancras take?
7. You want to visit Canterbury for the day. What two trains will you take?

St. Pancras / Canterbury West / St. Pancras – Summer 2015

St. Pancras depart	Canterbury West arrive	Canterbury West depart	St. Pancras arrive
8:33	9:29	16:07 ∞	17:07
9:05	10:08	16:37	17:36
9:37	10:35	17:05 *	17:52
10:01 *	10:53	17:37	18:35
10:40	11:50	18:12	19:19
11:07	12:05	18:50 +	20:02

* not Sunday
+ service to Charing Cross
∞ from Canterbury East

Answers:
1 10:01, 2 17:05, 3 18:50, 4 10:40, 5 16:07, 6 58 minutes, 7 ?

Idea for the Classroom: Quotes: The Tale of Thomas Becket

The tale of Thomas Becket is very dramatic and involves scenes of friendship, disagreement, anger and repenting. Can you identify who said these famous quotes: Thomas Becket, Henry II, the knights, Louis VII of France, or Edward Grimm (a bystander at Becket's death)? Look at the short explanations below for the answers.

1. *"Our friendship will turn to hate"*
2. *"If this is the chancellor's state, what can the king's be like?"*
3. *"Who will rid me of this troublesome priest?"*
4. *"Where is Thomas the traitor? Where is the archbishop?"* *"Here I am, no traitor, but archbishop and priest of God"*
5. *"The wicked knight leapt suddenly upon him, but still he stood firm and immovable. At the third blow he fell on his knees and elbows, offering himself a living sacrifice"*
6. *"For the name of Jesus and the protection of the Church, I am ready to embrace death"*
7. *"Touch me not... you and your accomplices act like madmen"*
8. *"Let us away, knights, this fellow will arise no more"*

Explanations:
1. Becket speaks to Henry II about Henry's insistence that Becket become Archbishop of Canterbury; he rightly thinks that their close friendship will be lost if Becket were to take this position.
2. King Louis VII of France speaks of Becket's wealth as Chancellor, saying that if the Chancellor leads such a luxurious lifestyle, then the King's lifestyle must be even better.

3. King Henry II is angry with Becket's interference in the royal courts, and that Becket excommunicated (threw out from the Church) several Archbishops.
4. The four knights arrive in Canterbury and ask the location of Becket, to which he replies that he is here, but that he is no traitor.
5. Edward Grimm gave an eyewitness account of the murder of Thomas Becket, and here he tells of how Becket fell to his knees.
6. Becket says this, realising that the knights have come to kill him.
7. Becket says this, claiming superiority over them because he is Archbishop, and tells them not to be crazy.
8. After the knights have murdered Becket, they flee with these words.

How about making some speech bubbles with these quotes to decorate your classroom walls? Look below – I've drawn an example.

Stained Glass Window

SAINT THOMAS BECKET

Thomas Becket: Speech Bubbles

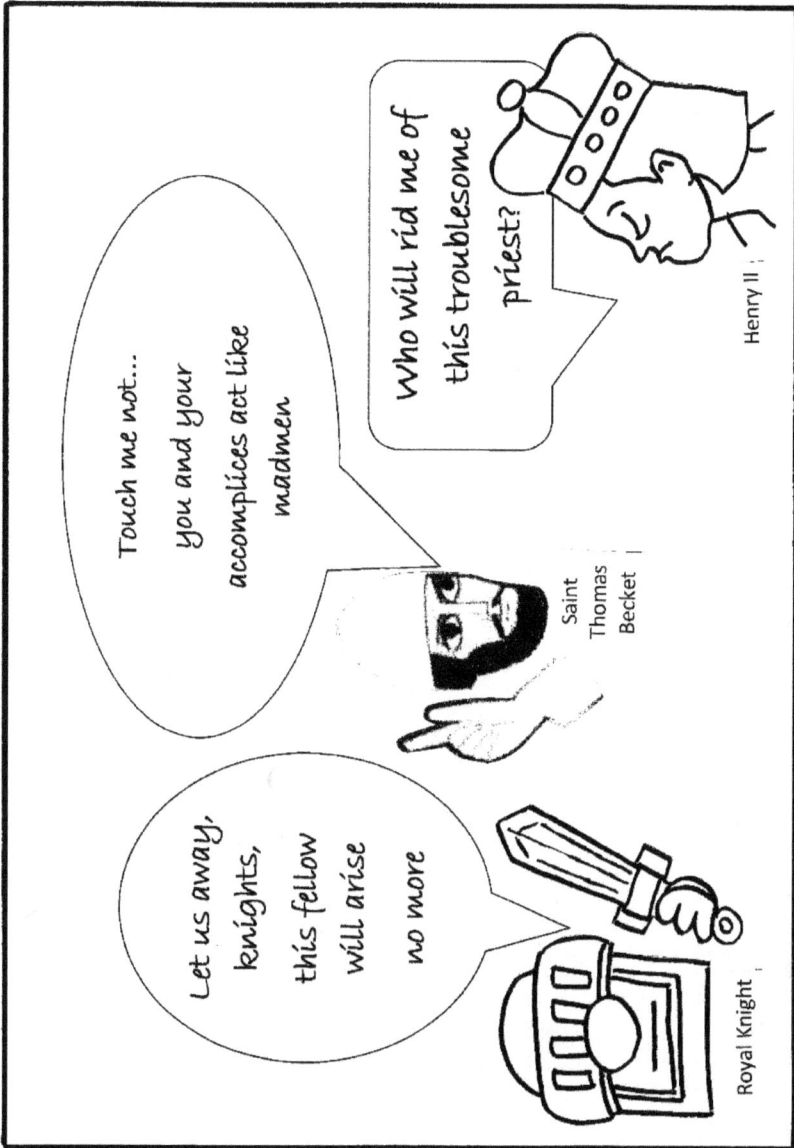

7.
SAINT CRISPIN'S DAY

BARRY NICHOLSON

7.
SAINT CRISPIN'S DAY

St Crispin's Day is the 25th October. It is a memorable day for the feast celebrating the twin saints Crispin and Crispinian, and for the many battles that occurred on that day, notably the Battle of Agincourt in 1415.

Crispin and Crispinian were two noble Roman brothers and legend has it that they were twins. They were missionaries of the Christian faith and went to Gaul to preach. They were very successful in their preaching, and also in their shoemaking which they carried on at night. The money they made paid for themselves and to aid the poor. However, the Governor of Gaul and Emperor Maximianus were jealous and had the twins tortured and then beheaded on 25th October in the year 285 or 286. They were made saints soon after their death, and are patron saints of shoemakers, cobblers and leatherworkers. The 25th October has become their 'Feast Day' in the religious calendar.

This day rings throughout history as the date of many battles. The most famous speech from the most famous battle to take place on this day is Shakespeare's St Crispin's Day Speech in the play *Henry V* (1599). Written nearly 200 years after the Battle of Agincourt, Shakespeare offers a fine dramatisation of the speech with themes of glory, fellowship and inspiration.

Henry V had led his men across northern France in an attempt to seize cities such as Harfleur and Calais that had once been English possessions. They hoped to get to Calais from where they could sail back to England. But there was a problem: the French army knew of Henry's plan, and knew that his army was much depleted. Estimates say the English soldiers were outnumbered 5 to 1. This did not go unnoticed by one of the soldiers, Westmoreland, and Henry's speech is provoked by Westmoreland's wish that they had more men fighting with them, "O that we now had here, But one ten thousand of those men in England, that do no work to-day!".

The French army moved between Henry's men and Calais preventing them from reaching the port, and daring them into a battle that they seemed doomed to lose. Montjoy, the French messenger, makes one last trip to the English camp to ask Henry if he wants to take the last opportunity to surrender. The offer is rejected, of course. But what could Henry and his men do? They knew the French knights were highly skilled, heavily armoured and greatly outnumbered them. Morale on the English side was low.

Henry V's strategy was to make a rousing speech, encouraging the men and expressing a belief that they would triumph. What followed (at least as Shakespeare dramatised it) was a masterful inspirational speech that ultimately led the English to victory. He dismissed that the smaller number of English fighters would be a disadvantage; that in victory "the fewer the men, the greater share of honour". He appealed to the soldiers' pride, saying that they would look back on the battle with spirit and boast "these wounds I had on St Crispin's Day" in the brave battle against the French. There is a proud call to unity with the speech's most famous line; "We few, we happy few, we band of brothers".

And so he inspires his men to victory. Using a combination of foot fighting and longbows he was able to plunge the French camp into disarray. Cunningham writes that the speech is Henry V's defining moment as a character, playing on themes of glory and fellowship. Although the speech is a work of fiction, it is a very memorable one in which Henry's strength of conviction and forceful personality come to the fore.

Cunningham elaborates on Henry V's personality: he has no friends in the play, and no emotional attachments of any kind. As shown in the speech, he is an effective public speaker and able to manipulate the emotional thinking of others – in this case his soldiers. He is himself a brave soldier, but somewhat emotionless and rigid. His pursuit of glory and of winning for its own sake, Cunningham writes, cuts him out as empty and, ultimately, selfish. Though a hero and victor at the play's end, the only beneficiary is himself.

2015 is the 600th anniversary of the Battle of Agincourt. There are several events planned to commemorate the battle. For me the most interesting is the St Crispin's Day Night Ride, an annual bicycle ride through the night past some of London's landmarks – including Tower Bridge. Their website encourages participants to "ride through the early hours… into the dawn of St Crispin's Day". The Night Ride started at one minute to midnight on Saturday 24th October, and the 100 mile or so ride will apparently took a maximum of sixteen hours. Participants got a 'ride passport', certificate, photo taken at the finish, and an Agincourt 600th anniversary hat. All proceeds go to charity.

Though the most famous is the Battle of Agincourt in 1415, some other notable battles took place on this day too. Foremost is the Battle of Balaclava (Charge of the Light Brigade) in the Crimean War, 1854. The battle is notable because, in contrast to Agincourt, it was a disaster. In World War II were the Second Battle of El Alamein (1942), the Battle of Henderson Field (1942), and the naval Battle of the Straits of Surigao. Add to these the Second Battle of Springfield, Missouri (1861), and the Battle of Marais des

Cygnes, Kansas (1864) amongst others, and we do seem to have a date predisposed to conflict.

To pay respect to Henry V it is possible to visit his burial site at Westminster Abbey in London. Henry has a lot of competition, though, as many of Britain's Kings and Queens are buried in the abbey, clustered around the High Altar. In fact, over 3,000 people are buried here in total, including royalty, statesmen, poets and writers, and scientists. Famed amongst the non-royalty are Geoffrey Chaucer (writer and poet) and the scientists Isaac Newton and Charles Darwin. More recently the funeral of Princess Diana and the wedding of Prince William and Catherine Middleton took place at the abbey, in 1997 and 2011 respectively.

Westminster Abbey is open Monday to Saturday from 9:30 to 3:30, and on Sunday and religious holidays for religious services only. Some people try to bypass the admission fee by looking round after one of the services – though this is not recommended. The nearest Underground stations are St James's Park and Westminster, and the nearest mainline stations are Victoria and Waterloo. From Waterloo there is an eye-catching walk across the Thames towards Big Ben and then Westminster Abbey beyond it, for which a camera is a necessity. But the main attraction for us is to remember Henry V and his brave band of brothers.

Idea for the Classroom: Bike Ride Entry Form

BARRY'S BIKE RIDE FOR CHARITY 2015

First name:
Last name:

Title: Mr Mrs Miss Dr Prof Rev Other
Gender: M F
Date of birth:
Address:
Postcode:
Mobile:
Meal choice: meat / veggie
Drink choice: cola / orange juice
Payment method: cash / debit card / credit card / PayPal
Write in less than 100 words why you would like to join the Bike
Ride:

> *I would like to join the Bike Ride because...*

If you win, you must make a short speech. What would you say?
(50 words)

> *Thank you. I want to say...*

Signature:
Today's date:

Filling in forms is an important skill, and in later life our students
will need to know how to fill out job applications, college
registration forms, or competition entry forms. Imagine you want
to take part in a charity cycle ride like the St Crispin's Day Night
Ride, and fill in your information in the form above. Be careful –
the last two sections require longer answers.

Idea for the Classroom: Famous Saints

Look at this list of famous saints. Do you know what they are the patron saint of, or what they are famous for? Try an internet search to find out more information but be careful – some of the saints have a lot more information about them than others, and a lot of the information is unknown or unspecified. When you have finished your list, you may like to cut the information out as cards to make a matching exercise.

Saint	Feast Day	Born / Died	Information
Thomas Becket	Dec. 29	b.1118 d.1170	In England recognized as protector of the Clergy.
Columba	June 9	b.521 d.597	Patron of Ireland, Scotland, floods, bookbinders, poets.
Crispin & Crispinian	Oct. 25	b.? d.285/286	Shakesspeare's St. Crispin's Day speech.
Pope John Paul II	Oct. 22	b.1920 d.2005	Patron of World Youth Day.
Thomas More	June 22	b.1478 d.1535	Patron of lawyers.
Nicholas	Dec. 6	b.? d.?	Patron of bakers and pawnbrokers; love of children.
Patrick	Mar. 17	b.387 d.461	Patron of Ireland; shamrock symbol.
Valentine	Feb. 14	b.? d.269	Patron of love, young people, happy marriages.

Idea for the Classroom: Henry V's Longbow Game

Henry V and his men won the battle not only because they were inspired by Henry's speech, but also because they used longbows, that could fire great distances very accurately. Now's your chance to test your longbow skills (and your luck!) in Henry V's Longbow Game.

Make up a board or use the one below, and find enough counters or coins (to represent eighteen soldiers on each team) and a dice.

There are two teams, who take it in turn to roll the dice and move one of their soldiers that number of spaces and hopefully 'hit' an opponent's soldier. For example, if Henry's team throw a six, they could 'hit' any of the French soldiers; but if they throw a one, two or three, their arrow falls in to no man's land and they hit none of the enemy. Soldiers can only move forwards, not diagonally, horizontally or backwards.

As the game progresses, it becomes more difficult to hit the opponent's soldiers. The team to hit all the enemy's men first is the winner. Hooray!

Henry V's Longbow Game

Henry V's Army

NO MAN'S LAND

NO MAN'S LAND

NO MAN'S LAND

French Army

8.
HADRIAN'S
WALL
OF
EMPIRE

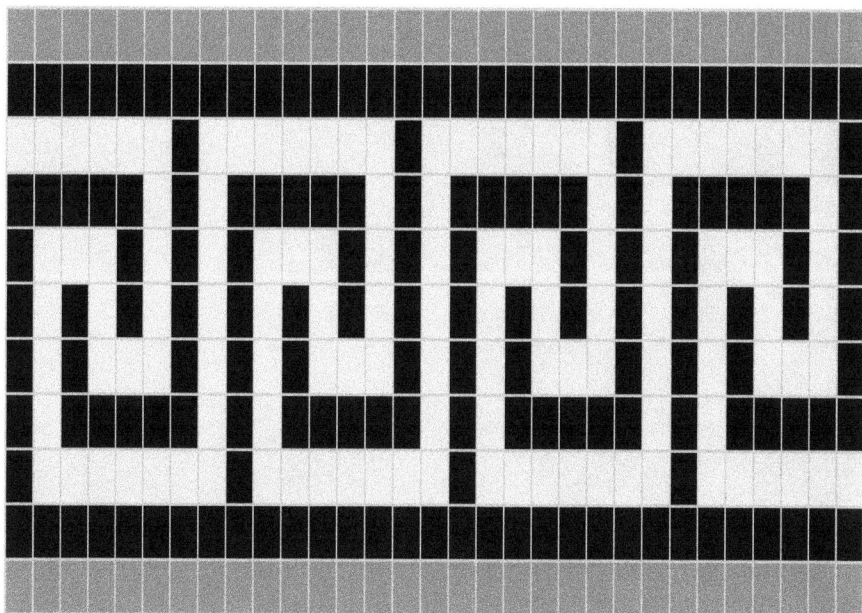

8.
HADRIAN'S WALL
OF EMPIRE

One of the greatest structures of the Roman Empire is Hadrian's Wall in northern England. Stretching 118 km (74 miles), it marks the northern boundary of what was the great Roman Empire, from Wallsend in the east to Bowness in the west. In addition to the wall there are numerous fortifications, gatehouses, turrets and settlements which combine to give the visitor a pleasurable day trip.

Emperor Hadrian (Publius Aelius Hadrianus) was born in Spain on January 24th AD76. At the age of fourteen he began his military training and on August 11th AD117 he became emperor. He visited Britain in AD122 and, sensing the need to mark the boundary of the empire, and with imminent military threats, ordered construction of the wall.

Construction began soon after Hadrian's visit. It was carefully mapped and planned; milecastles and turrets were built first, then the wall was built to join them up. For much of its course it followed the natural boundary of Whin Sill, a ragged line of cliffs stretching across the country. In total eleven forts were built, six of them astride the wall and five nearby it. It was extended east to Wallsend, and was completed by AD128.

The wall was designed to be of stone, three metres wide and four and a half metres high, and with a total distance of 118 km (74 miles). In fact, much of the wall was initially built in turf, with sloping sides six metres (20ft) wide at the base. At every Roman mile there was a large fortified gateway (milecastle) with accommodation for a dozen or more soldiers. Between each milecastle were two turrets (watchtowers). To the north of the wall ran a deep ditch (3 metres / 10 ft deep) and to the south a Vallum, or flat-bottomed ditch, six metres wide. The purpose of the Vallum was probably to create a protected military zone, and to control access to the south. Construction of the ditch and Vallum were abandoned where the rock was too hard for excavation. Finally, between the Vallum and the wall was the 'Military Way' or military road running the length of the wall.

What was the wall built for? Its exact purpose is still undecided, but there is no doubt that it helped Roman soldiers monitor movements of people and goods in and out of the empire: traffic could be searched and taxed before being allowed to continue. In military terms, it was to defend against incursions by raiders, and it was also good for relaying messages from one post to another. Importantly, the wall marked the edge of the empire and clearly reminded people in their minds about the might of Rome.

An interesting interpretation of the wall is offered by Johnson (1990) who suggests that it hindered the Romans as much as it was a help. For instance, it did not aid Roman mobility but was a barrier to it; it did not adequately control movements of people or goods as these were both smuggled across in numbers; and importantly that the wall expressed an admission of failure on the part of the Romans – it marked the edge of the empire and its dreams for expansion.

In AD296 troops were removed from the wall to return to the continent, and by AD410 Rome had stopped sending money to support troops in Britain. The wall entered a period of steady decline, and by the mid fourteenth century much of the wall and its forts had fallen into disrepair.

Chesters Roman Fort is a good example of one of the many forts built along or nearby the wall's course. It was chosen as a site because it is where Hadrian's Wall crosses the River Tyne, though the wall itself is no longer visible here. Chesters is one of the best preserved examples of a Roman cavalry fort in Britain, and was constructed soon after the wall was first built in AD122-3.

As is typical of a Roman fort, it is rectangular in shape, about half as long as it is wide, measuring 175 by 130 metres, and within an area of 5.7 acres. The walls are mostly of stone, and some turf-and-timber, surrounded by a V-shaped ditch running parallel to them. There were four gates, two in the middle of the shorter sides and two about a third of the way along the longer sides. The gates were the starting points of streets running through the fort. There were four towers, one at each of the four rounded corners. In the central area were administration buildings, including a headquarters building and the commanding officer's house. In the other areas was accommodation for troops, and stores. It was a very busy and crowded place: all areas within the fort would have been covered with roads and buildings.

The most notable remains at Chesters is the bathhouse, situated outside the fort itself because of the risk of fire from the furnaces that provided hot air for heating the bathhouse. An aqueduct brought in a constant supply of water; waste was sent straight into the Tyne.

The baths were first excavated in 1884-5, and photos of the time by J.P. Gibson show them in a remarkable state of preservation, just as they are today. They consisted a series of rooms for different treatments and of different temperatures. The first room after entering the building was the changing room with seven niches for statues representing the seven days of the week.

The latrine had wooden seats suspended over a deep channel, and there were also rooms for a hot bath, cold bath, and steam treatments. In the hot, dry room not only the floor but also the walls were heated by the circulation of hot air. As the floors in many of the rooms were very hot, it was customary to wear sandals whilst bathing.

Conforming with the typical fortress plan, Chesters is rectangular-shaped with four gates. I find the gates very interesting because they had two arched doors each, complemented with strong oak gates, with small guard rooms on either side. The gates would have been as much as ten metres high, the best preserved of which is the East Gate. Though not nearly ten metres high, the gate clearly shows the foundations and lower walling of the double gate, complete with guard rooms either side.

Vindolanda Roman Fort follows the same basic pattern, but was constructed in the late AD80s before Hadrian's Wall was built in order to protect the busy Stanegate Road. It was first excavated by Anthony Hedley in the 1830s. At first the fort was built in timber and turf, but was later rebuilt in stone. It was home for up to 500 soldiers.

Vindolanda also has a bath house, big enough to hold around fifty people and used by all who lived in Vindolanda. Just like at Chesters, the baths were heated by hot air circulating under the floors, and the house itself was located outside the fort because of risk of fire.

Other important features at Vindolanda are the wells and water tanks which serviced fresh water to the fort via a series of stone aqueducts and timber pipes. Visitors can also see the remnants of the commanding officer's house and the headquarters building. The former was where the commanding officer and his family lived, enjoying their own baths and entertainment rooms. The latter was a very busy place with a chapel, strongroom, and the 'long room' used for assemblies.

On a final note is the museum, established in 1831 by the site's first archaeologist Anthony Hedley. The most famous exhibits are the Vindolanda Writing Tablets, the discovery of which made Vindolanda one of the most important military sites in the Roman Empire. Wooden tablets like these from AD90-105 rarely survive. They include work rotas, official letters, private letters, and official reports. One of the tablets, for example, requests money to pay for grain; another for the urgent loan of an axe; and a memorable tablet giving a birthday invitation.

In 1970 the Vindolanda Trust was established to excavate and preserve the site. A more recent addition in the vicinity has been the opening of the Roman Army Museum in 1981, which houses a fine collection of artefacts and reconstructions.

Getting to Hadrian's Wall is relatively easy as it extends over such a large area of northern England, although a lot of the wall in the east is non-existent: the ravages of centuries plus Newcastle's urban sprawl have eaten away at it. Nevertheless, central Newcastle has a couple of historic sites of interest including Segedunum Roman Fort in Wallsend and, lost in the city, the remains of Newcastle Keep. From the battlements here there are great views over the River Tyne in both directions. Near the other end of the wall in Carlisle is another castle and a handful of museums.

Most worthwhile for a visit is the central section and forts, including Chesters, Vindolanda and Housesteads. There is a handy bus, the 'AD122 Hadrian's Wall Country Bus' that runs the course of the wall from April to September. It connects to mainline rail or regular bus services at Carlisle, Haltwhistle, Walltown or Hexam. The bus stops at frequent intervals with a number of pubs (serving food) on the route. The publicity at visithadrianswall.co.uk advises to "leave the car at home and discover.. the Hadrian's Wall Heritage Site by using the award winning AD122 Country Bus service". Look at this site for exact timetables and connections. A discounted 'Rover' ticket is available.

Serious walkers can tackle the Hadrian's Wall Trail, 135 km long (and so 17 km longer than the wall itself). Maps and guides are available at many places. Keep an eye on the weather as the sites are exposed and offer little in the way of shelter; Moffat (2008) notes that if the weather is bad it must be "a long, head-down slog" to walk some sections of the route.

Tourist facilities at the sites are good, with maps and interpretation in abundance, plus the obligatory souvenir shops. Other than small on-site cafes and the few pubs along the route there is little in the way of refreshment, so a packed lunch is a good idea.

Whatever part of the wall is visited, we are given a wonderful window onto the Roman way of life at this far-flung part of their empire. Hadrian, who died in AD138, has left us with one of the most interesting and complete assemblies of Roman architecture in the world. I wonder what he would think about the new army of day trippers and tourists visiting his great fortresses and wall?

Idea for the Classroom: Hadrian's Wall Timeline

Look at the Hadrian's Wall Timeline below. Can you write an event for each of the dates? All the answers are in the text, and the first one is done for you. If you can't wait then you can cheat by looking at the answers in a few pages' time.

AD	event
43	*Roman invasion of Britain*
76	
80s	
90	
90-105	
117	
122	
122-3	
128	
138	
296	
410	
1830s	
1831	
1884-5	
1970	
1981	

Idea for the Classroom: Country Code / Code of Respect

When visiting the countryside it is always important to observe the Country Code, and in addition to this at Hadrian's Wall there is also 'Hadrian's Wall Code of Respect'.

Look at the summary of the Country Code below. Try to re-write the rules using a modal verb (should, must, have to, can't, etc), for example "You must always follow the Country code":

- Always follow the Country Code
- Be safe – plan ahead and follow any signs
- Leave gates and property as you find them
- Protect plants and animals, and take your litter home
- Keep dogs under close control
- Consider other people

Now take a look at the Hadrian's wall Code of Respect, and again try to re-write the rules using modal verbs:

- Never climb or walk on top of the wall (except for a short section at Housesteads)
- Take pressure off the wall itself by going to a Roman fort as part of your visit
- Only walk along the signed and waymarked paths
- Dogs must be kept on a lead
- Take litter away with you
- Never light fires
- Close all gates behind you unless it is clear that the farmer needs the gate to be left open
- In wet winter months the ground is waterlogged and suffers greatest damage from our feet, so try to visit a Roman fort like Chesters or Vindolanda instead.

Idea for the Classroom: Roman Mosaic

The Romans liked to decorate their floors with beautiful mosaics with representations of historical scenes, battles, hunting, or animals. Below I have provided the outlines for two mosaics plus a grid that can be coloured and cut into squares then stuck on the outlines. Alternatively cut out your own squares from colourful glossy magazines. Use these outlines or try and find some images of your own; be creative – the mosaics could be A4 size, or they might be several square metres!

Answers:

AD	event
43	Roman invasion of Britain
76	Hadrian born
80s	Vindolanda Roman Fort constructed
90	Hadrian began his military training
90-105	Date of Vindolanda wooden tablets
117	Hadrian became Emperor
122	Hadrian visited Britain
122-3	Chesters Roman Fort constructed
128	Hadrian's Wall completed
138	Hadrian died
296	Troops removed from wall
410	Rome stops sending money to Britain
1830s	Vindolanda first excavated
1831	Museum at Vindolanda established
1884-5	Chesters: baths first excavated
1970	Vindolanda Trust established
1981	Roman Army Museum opened

Roman Mosaic A

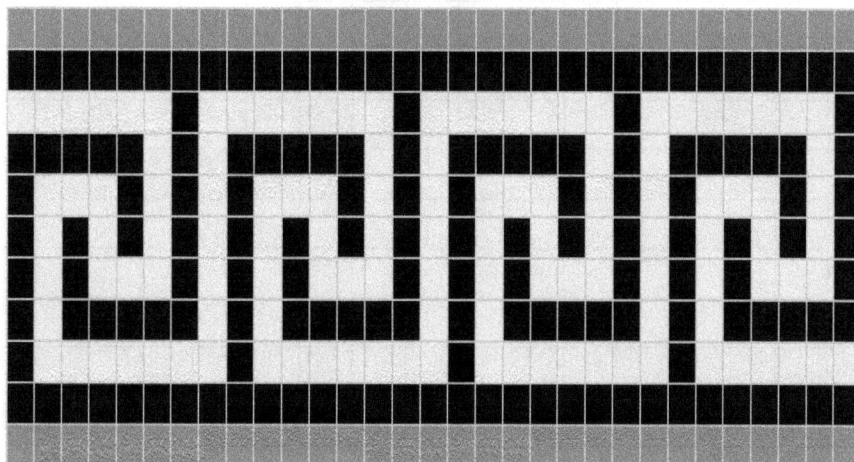

Roman Mosaic B

Mosaic Squares

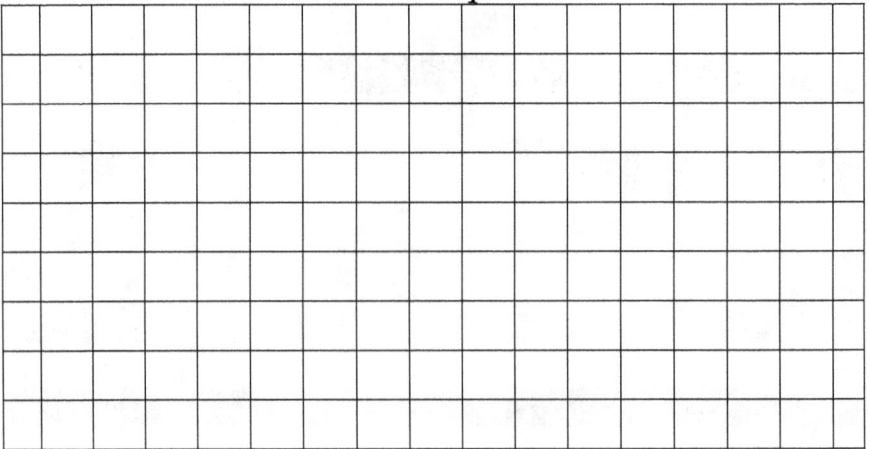

9.
A TALE
OF
TWO
DRAGONS

9.
A TALE OF TWO DRAGONS

Dragons have a powerful meaning as they represent not only strength and power but also destruction. Taking their place in mythology are two important British dragons: the poisonous dragon that Saint George killed, and the proud Welsh dragon.

The dragon motif is of Eastern origin, and the first tales of dragons were brought back during the Crusades. Early appearances of the dragon motif were in tenth century Cappadocia and eleventh century Georgia. Since those times the dragon legend has gradually become part of Christian traditions and festivals.

Let's take two dragon tales in turn – first Saint George and the dragon that he famously slayed, and second the Welsh dragon as represented on the Welsh national flag. The two are not dissimilar as both rely on myth and have some doubt as to their origins, and both are the subject of strong national pride.

Saint George is the patron saint of England and Saint George's Day is 23rd April. He is identified with the English ideals of honour, bravery and gallantry. We think of him as dressed in a white tunic with a red cross, upon his horse, spearing a dragon as he rescues a fair maiden. But in fact a lot of information about him is dubious and blurred and very little is known about the man himself. The fact that he was not English has become blurred into mythology.

Nonetheless, he has a lot to do with English identity and represents an up to date version of an older pagan myth. We know he was born in Cappadocia (in modern-day Turkey) in the third century AD, and that his parents were Christian. He became a Roman soldier but protested Rome's persecution of Christians and resigned his military post in protest. Because of this he was imprisoned and finally beheaded, but he always stayed true to his faith.

Saint George became a well-known name in 1483 with the printing of the book *The Golden Legend* which was an account of various saints' lives. *The Golden Legend* revolves around a town called Silene in Libya, a sufficiently exotic location for a dragon to live. The story goes that the town had a lake in which a plague-bearing creature lived. He was a poisonous beast, and poisoned much of the surrounding countryside. To appease the dragon, locals fed him two sheep each day. However, when they ran out of sheep they started to feed it their own people out of fear. They were to be chosen by lottery.

One day the lot fell on the King's daughter, Sabra. Of course the King did not like this and tried to bargain his way out of the situation. Distraught with grief, he offered the people all his gold, silver and treasure and half his kingdom to spare his daughter... but the people refused. Reluctantly the King dressed his daughter in bridal clothes and sent her to the lake to await her fate.

By chance Saint George was riding by and, hearing her story, vowed to help her. As the dragon reared out of the lake, George held up the sign of the cross and charged the dragon on horseback, giving it a mighty wound with his spear. He called to the princess to throw him her girdle which he put around the dragon's neck. Amazingly, the dragon followed the girl around "like a meek beast on a leash".

The dragon was led back to Silene but the people there were frightened at the terrifying sight. George called to the locals saying that if they consented to becoming Christians he would slay the dragon before them. They agreed, converted to Christianity, and George obligingly slew the dragon before their very eyes. The body of the beast was so large that it had to be taken away on four ox carts. On the site where the dragon was slain, the King built a church dedicated to the Blessed Virgin Mary and Saint George. The church became a site of pilgrimage because from its altar came a spring whose waters were said to cure all disease.

A variation tells that Saint George had spent many months travelling when he finally arrived in Libya. He met a poor hermit who told him that everyone in their land was in great danger from a dragon. Apparently the dragon demanded the daily sacrifice of a beautiful maiden and now only the King's daughter remained. Indeed, the King offered his daughter's hand in marriage for anyone who could slay the dragon.

So, at daybreak George set out to the valley where the dragon lived. The dragon, upon seeing George, rushed from its cave roaring with a sound louder than thunder. It's tail alone was said to be fifty feet long. George bravely struck the creature with his spear. Unfortunately the spear broke into a thousand pieces because the dragon's scales were so hard. George fell from his horse but fortunately he rolled under an enchanted orange tree. The dragon's poison couldn't harm him and he was able to recover and fight again. With his sword in his hand, he rushed at the dragon and pierced it under its wing where there were no protective scales. The dragon fell dead.

Another version tells that Saint George initially loses his battle against the dragon and that he retreats to a nearby river. He prays, and removes his armour in order to melt it down. He takes the melted metal and forges it into a box into which he places his fears, doubts and lack of faith. He now faces the dragon again and this time instantly slays the beast.

Whichever version is preferred, the story of Saint George gained popularity in England in the fourteenth and fifteenth centuries. Edward III was an enthusiastic early supporter and in 1348 he picked George as a special patron of the Order of the Garter and dedicated the chapel at Windsor Castle in the saint's honour. Edward III proclaimed Saint George as "the most invincible athlete of Christ, whose name and protection the English nation invoke as that of their patron, especially in war". It was around this time that the legend moved to the mainstream of English society. His flag – a red cross on a white background – can be seen all over England today.

Moving on, there is one other dragon in Britain that evokes national feeling and inspires cultural identity: the Welsh Dragon ("Y Ddraig Goch") as symbolised on the Welsh flag. Interestingly, Wales is not represented on the UK's Union Flag but has its own flag consisting a red dragon on a green and white background. It was first used as a symbol of Wales in AD 829 and became the proud and ancient battle standard of Celtic leaders such as King Arthur. It is a symbol of national identity and all things Welsh and is used by many public and private institutions. It is claimed to be the oldest national flag still in use.

The tale of the Welsh Dragon first appeared in a collection of eleven stories, the *Mabinogion*, in which a red (Welsh) dragon fights an invading white (English) dragon. Lludd, the King of Britain, asked his wise brother Llefelys for advice. He told Lludd to dig a pit in the centre of Britain, fill it with mead and cover it with cloth. As expected the dragons drank the mead and fell asleep.

Lludd imprisoned them in Dinas Emrys in Snowdonia where the dragons remained trapped for centuries.

After this time, the King Vortigern tried to build a castle on the site. However every night the castle walls and foundations were demolished by unseen forces (we know it was the dragons). Vortigern consulted his advisors who told him to find an orphan boy and sacrifice him, allowing him to build his castle. He chose a boy (who was later to become Merlin) who on hearing he is to be sacrificed tells the King the story of the red and white dragons. The King was convinced and excavated the area which in turn released the two dragons. The red and white dragon continued their fight until the red dragon finally won.

The boy tells the King that the white dragon symbolises the Saxons (English) and the red dragon symbolises the people of Vortigern (later to become the Welsh). The Welsh dragon defeated the English dragon, and that's why the dragon is such a proud and revered symbol of Wales.

That's also why the dragon is on the flag of Wales. The Welsh flag as we know it was first used at the Battle of Bosworth Field in 1485, when Henry Tudor defeated Richard III. The dragon motif was brought to England by the House of Tudor that held the English throne from 1485 until 1603. Henry VII (the first Tudor king) added the green and white stripes to the flag. It was not until 1807, however, that the dragon design was recognised by the British parliament.

Interestingly, the heraldic use of the dragon was common throughout Europe, though Wales is the only nation to keep the image on its national flag. Similar to China and the East, the dragon is seen as a positive symbol in contrast to elsewhere in Europe. Today the Welsh Dragon continues to be a positive and proud symbol.

Any visitor to Wales will see the dragon motif everywhere, especially atop castles and public buildings. The same can be said for Saint George's flag in England, though it has competition from its brother, the Union Flag.

Idea for the Classroom: Flags

Every country in the world has a flag as a symbol of national identity. In this tale we have seen Saint George's flag used by England (a red cross on a white background) and the red dragon flag used by Wales (a red dragon on a white and green background).

How about making a flag of your own? Think about shapes, animals, plants, people and things when you are planning your design. I've given you a few ideas below together with some blank templates. Have fun!

Idea for the Classroom: Fortunately – Unfortunately

This is a speaking game that forces players to 'argue' using the starting words *fortunately* and *unfortunately* with the aim of building up a story. Pairs take it in turns to say *fortunately* then *unfortunately* sentences. Start the story off and continue in a similar manner to this:

> ➢ *Fortunately it was a sunny day so my Gran went for a walk.*

> ➢ *Unfortunately it started to rain.*

> ➢ *Fortunately she had her umbrella with her.*

> ➤ *Unfortunately the umbrella had a big hole in it.*

> ➤ *Fortunately it stopped raining.*

> ➤ *Unfortunately it started to snow.*

> ➤ *Fortunately my Gran likes the snow.*

> ➤ *Unfortunately she slipped on the ice.*

> ➤ *Fortunately she didn't hurt herself…* and so on…

Idea for the Classroom: Design your own Monster

What physical features does a monster such as a dragon have? The Welsh Dragon has four legs, two wings and a fearsome head, but dragons from Turkey or China are snake-like, without legs, and may resemble a serpent. So there are lots of ways to describe your creature and here are some ideas:

body part	description
head and face	*large, small, circular, oval, long, thin, ugly, fearsome, spectacular, fire-breathing*
body	*fat, thin, bulging, snake-like, serpent-like, skinny*
legs	*long, short, stumpy, broad, thin, flippers, bendy knees, hairy*
tail	*long, short, sword-tipped, axe-tipped, pointy, swaying from side to side*
personality	*angry, fierce, firey, dangerous, never-ending, attacking*

There are a couple of ways to approach this in the classroom. First as a describe and draw activity where the teacher describes the monster for the students to draw. Start with the body, move on to the face and then the other body parts – legs, wings, tail and so on. The monsters can be drawn in secret and revealed at the end with humorous results.

A second way is to make a model of your monster from rubbish such as old cardboard, egg boxes and yoghurt pots. For the body you can use cardboard rolled or folded into shape; the legs could be yoghurt pots; the neck and head made from a cereal packet and yoghurt pot; humps on its back made with parts of an egg carton; and wings made of either card or cloth. Tape or stick the lot together and either use oil-based or spray paint to paint it. When it's dry, add finishing touches such as beady eyes, claws, scales, and crepe paper to represent fire. Roar!

Ideas for Flags

Design idea 1

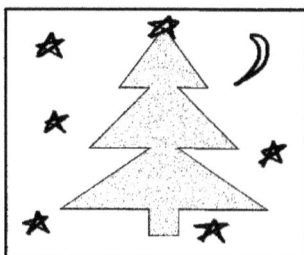

Design idea 2

Design idea 3

Your designs...

BARRY NICHOLSON

10.
STONEHENGE:
CIRCLES
IN
STONE

BARRY NICHOLSON

10.
STONEHENGE: CIRCLES IN STONE

Stonehenge, a UNESCO World Heritage site since 1986, covers nearly 1000,000 acres and is perhaps the most important prehistoric structure in the world. One might be forgiven for thinking, then, that the place has been well-managed over the centuries. Well, yes and no.

The history of the management of Stonehenge has been choppy to say the least, with many twists and turns and changes of fortune, involving a large number of stakeholders including English Heritage (which owns the main site), the National Trust (which owns a lot of the land around the stones), archaeologists, Druids and religious groups, conservationists, local residents, the military, the Department of Transport, the Royal Society for the Protection of Birds, UNESCO... you get the point: a lot of people have an interest in Stonehenge.

In this chapter I want to look at Stonehenge not so much in relation to its history, but in terms of how it has been preserved and managed, its visitor-friendly-ness, and attempts to improve it. How have archaeologists treated the site? What attractions and attempts at visitor interpretation have been made? And how has the area been affected by the building of roads and car parks?

Going back in time to the early 1900s, it was becoming increasingly obvious that something had to be done about Stonehenge, and in the following decades what this 'something' should be has been the subject of often heated debate. The first reaction in the early 1900s was to put up a fence of barbed wire around the site and charge an admission charge, on the recommendation of Sir Edmund Antrobus. Understandably, this action was very controversial and amounted, some claimed, to 'enclosure'.

The activities of archaeologists have been similarly doubtful. Though early excavations from 1901 were professional and undertaken with the eyes of experience, later excavations by W. Hawley in the late 1920s were less so: some of the leaning stones were put straight and set in concrete, and in general the excavations led to the discovery of little of interest. Hill (2008) writes that a great deal of 'irreversible damage' was done around that time.

By the late 1920s there was a notable increase in visitor numbers – especially by car. Road traffic became a problem at Stonehenge for the first time, especially after 1935 when the first car park was built. The architect C. Williams-Ellis noted that by the late 1920s the situation had become 'intolerable' with blots on the landscape including a café, turnstile and kiosk, spiked iron railings, and the derelict hangars of an aerodrome.

The hangars and military huts were a remnant of preparations for World War I, as there was a rush to construct military installations and runways. It was not just concrete building that affected the solitude of Stonehenge, but also army manoeuvres that churned the soil and made the ground shake. The area around Stonehenge was filled with tanks, huts and ammunition dumps.

The first serious restoration of the stones began in 1958, as stones were re-erected, straightened and re-set, in an effort to put right earlier attempts at restoration. By 1963 the last stone had been re-set. It was stressed from then on that improvements should have 'safety' and 'good display' at their core.

We pick up the Stonehenge saga in the early 1990s when the site attracted over 600,000 people a year. In those days, despite the work in the 1950s and 1960s, the reinforced fence remained, the roads were busy, the car park overflowing, and the visitor centre in need of re-vamping. It was generally agreed that the roads were priority, especially the A344 and A303 that run by the site. The question was: should the roads be moved, or buried in a tunnel?

In 1999 the 'Stonehenge Master Plan' was launched in an attempt to find an organisation or company to redesign and run the Stonehenge site. It proposed burying the A303 in a cut and cover tunnel, and the opening of a new visitor centre alongside a complex of shops and restaurants. A firm of Australian architects won the contract, and their plan revolved around a new visitor centre that would blend into the landscape. Backed by the Department of the Environment, the plan was disappointing, and eventually came to nothing.

Two further proposals were forthcoming. First, the Department of Transport announced a 2.1km bored tunnel. Though the tunnel idea was supported by English Heritage, others objected because the tunnel entrances were still too close to the stones. The second proposal was in 2004-5 when English Heritage applied for planning permission for a new visitor centre. However, in 2007 the government decided the bored tunnel was too expensive, and with it the visitor centre plans were abandoned too.

There were proposals for a temporary visitor centre during the 2012 London Olympics, and it seems from the new Stonehenge website (see English-heritage.org.uk) that they've finally got their act together. The website invites us to "walk in the footsteps of our Neolithic ancestors... step inside the Neolithic houses to discover everyday Neolithic life (and) visit the world-class exhibition and visitor centre". I'm particularly impressed by the looks of the 'Standing in the Stones' 3D film experience, a milestone in site interpretation. Special events are now being planned throughout the year, too.

With all this renewed interest and activity I might suggest nearby Woodhenge as a quieter option; whilst the overall impression is less dramatic, it is more atmospheric, feels less chopped about, and there are far fewer sightseers!

Stonehenge is open every day from 9:30 to 7pm except Christmas Day, and visiting is fairly easy. The nearest railway station is Salisbury, about nine miles. From here the Wiltshire and Dorset Bus Company service number 3 runs to the site (see morebus.co.uk). There is a visitor centre but don't get excited.

If you're in the area for longer than a day then there are two museums of interest. The first is the Salisbury and South Wiltshire Museum in Cathedral Square in Salisbury which houses numerous finds from Stonehenge. The second is the Devizes Museum which includes Celtic relics and some fine watercolours.

Who knows the final fate of Stonehenge? My hope is that it remains a monument to our ancestors and that an effective plan for managing the site and its visitors can be found. To me this means re-routing the nearby roads, possibly in tunnels, and the provision of a quality visitor centre and interpretation at the site, following successful examples elsewhere in the country. A good start has been made by English Heritage recently. But keeping the numerous stakeholders happy is sure to be the main stumbling block in this process.

Idea for the Classroom: Stakeholders

Stakeholders are people or groups that hold an interest in something, usually a controversial topic or issue. Stonehenge is a classic example of how the various stakeholder's views have got in the way of each other proving the old adage that 'too many cooks spoil the broth'.

See how many different stakeholders you can identify from the information above, and write them into the blank chart. I have started to fill the information in for you, and in a few pages is my version of the completed chart (don't cheat!).

stakeholder	background information and view on the development of Stonehenge
UNESCO	• *made Stonehenge a World Heritage Site in 1986* • *concerned for the maintenance of the fabric and historical quality of the site*
English Heritage	

Idea for the Classroom: Cardboard Stonehenge

If travelling to Stonehenge is too much of a task, why not bring the mountain to Moses? With a plentiful supply of cardboard and a large enough space (preferably outdoors) your students can try to build a Stonehenge. This cardboard Stonehenge can be used as a special display at a parent's evening or school fair.

Preparation is essential with this activity: your first job is to locate a number of equally-sized cardboard boxes from your local supermarket or recycling point. They don't have to be *exactly* the same size as the ravages of time have made the real Stonehenge uneven. What you do need to do is check that there are no hidden staples or attachments that could make the boxes unsafe.

OK, so you now have a large collection of equally-sized and safe boxes. What next? Start to place the vertical 'stones' in a circle, as large as you can make it. Place other 'stones' across the tops to make the distinctive Stonehenge shape. Arrange them in a circular pattern similar to this:

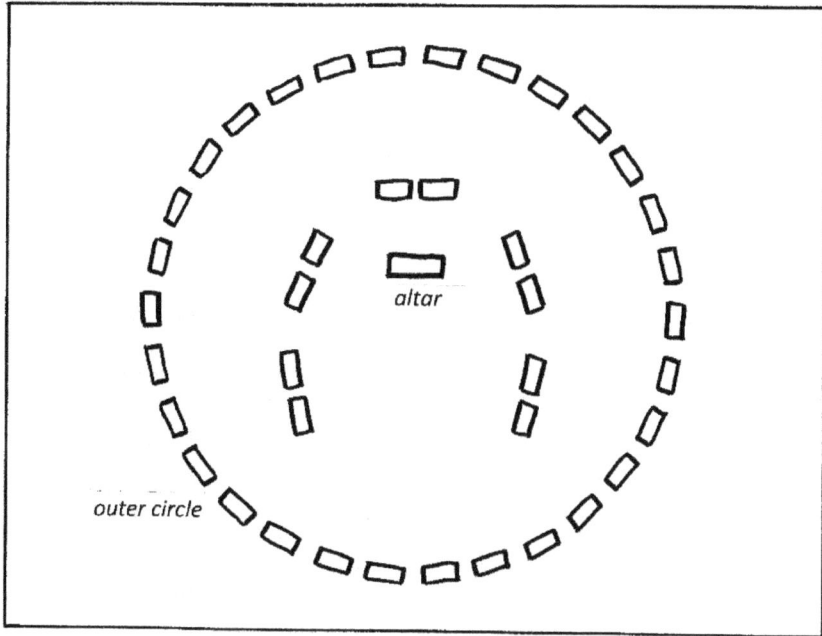

altar

outer circle

Idea for the Classroom: Stone Painting

This is a simple craft activity that primary children will enjoy. Collect some smooth and rounded stones from the garden, river or beach. Make sure that you clean them well and that they are free of mud and weed. Use oil-based paint to decorate them: animals and flowers are popular themes. When finished the stones can be used as paper weights or door stops, or simply by themselves to liven up a desk or shelf.

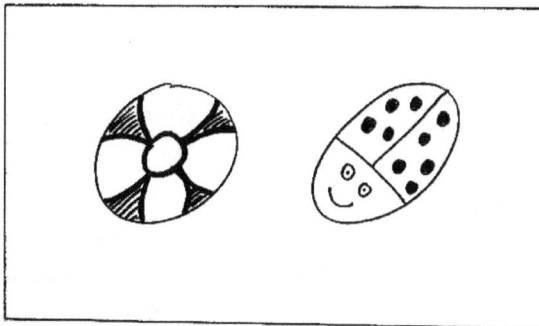

Stakeholders: Completed Chart:

stakeholder	background information and view on the development of Stonehenge
UNESCO	• *made Stonehenge a World Heritage Site in 1986* • *concerned for the maintenance of the fabric and historical quality of the site*
English Heritage	• *owns the main site* • *backed the Department of Transport plan for a tunnel in early 200s* • *2004-5 applied for permission for a new visitor centre – abandoned* • *finally got government backing for a visitor centre in 2012*
National Trust	• *owns a lot of the land around the stones* • *concerned about the historical and environmental quality of the site*
archaeologists	• *doubtful activities, historically (eg. stones set in concrete)* • *later attempts at restoration (since the late 1950s) more successful*
Druids	• *say the site is of religious and ceremonial significance, especially the Summer Solstice* • *access for them has at times been restricted*
conservationists	• *say the tunnel options may cause more damage than not* • *note the effect of roads and tunnels on birds and wildlife*

the military	• has historically used the area for tanks, huts and ammunition dumps • has remained quieter recently
government departments	• Department of the Environment backed a 'Stonehenge Master Plan' in 1999 – ultimately unsuccessful • Department of Transport announced a 2.1km tunnel in the early 2000s – it was never built
local residents	• concerned that new roads and tunnels will affect their quality of life, community, and property prices
visitors and day trippers	• large numbers have been visiting since the late 1920s • new visitor centre opened in 2012

11.
BANKSY'S DISMALAND

11.
BANKSY'S DISMALAND

Banksy is a famous street artist in Britain whose art is urban and graffiti inspired. His latest work is a theme park that is dreary and dismal on purpose.

Banksy is the pseudonym of a graffiti street artist whose identity is unknown. He was probably born in Bristol, England in 1973/4. His style is characterised by sarcastic and striking images, often involving animals, people, and personalities. Commonly his works are on display on streets, walls, bridges and buildings, and they are often powerful and controversial in theme.

The origins of Banksy's work was with the graffiti crew called DBZ (DryBreadZ) in the Bristol area. In the mid-1990s he started to use his trademark stencil technique, using several layers of stenciling combined with spray paint. Things really took off when the artwork started to sell at Sotheby's of London: a stencil of the Mona Lisa with paint dripping from her eyes sold for £57,000 in 2006; *Space Girl and Bird* sold for £288,000 the following year. People started to talk of 'The Banksy Effect' as high prices were paid for his work and other artists started to be influenced by his style.

Examples of his influential work and exhibitions include: *Turf War* (2003), London, which featured painted animals; *Barely Legal* (2006), Los Angeles, with an elephant painted in a floral pattern; *Banksy vs Bristol Museum* (2009), Bristol, his last exhibition until recently; *Exit Through the Gift Shop* (2010), a documentary film; New York (2013), where he created a new artwork for each day of his residency, and sold art on the street for a low $60 each; *Dismaland* (2015), his latest exhibition.

But who is he? Nobody knows for sure. Even his family doesn't know. But one name that crops up more than others is Robin Gunningham, born in Bristol in 1974, and who moved to London around the year 2000 which fits into Banksy's timeline. Still, the infamous artist refuses to be interviewed, and it has even been suggested that he is a woman, or a team of seven artists.

Dismaland, a 'bemusement park' set up in Western-super-Mare, is Banksy's latest attempt and his first UK show in six years. Billed as a "family theme park unsuitable for children", it's the kind of place that you either love or hate.

The site is a former pleasure swimming pool on the seafront at Western-super-Mare in Somerset. The *Tropicana* lido was built in 1937 but fell into disuse in 2000 and lay derelict for fifteen years until the summer of 2015 when something unusual started to happen. Amongst great secrecy, the locals were told that a Hollywood film company, Atlas Entertainment, was preparing to film for a crime thriller called Grey Fox. When pictures of the site began to surface on the internet in early August 2015, suspicions were aroused that this was more than a film set, and as the fairy castle and sculptures began to be erected, the purpose of the site became gradually less secret.

Finally, on August 22nd, the pop-up art exhibition was revealed and the 2.5 acre site opened to the public. What lay before visitors was a grimy dystopian theme park with a "demented assortment of bizarre and beautiful artworks" (from thisiscolossal.com) centred round a decaying version of Cinderella's castle similar in style to the Disney castle. Inside the castle was the truly dismal scene of Cinderella's chariot crash with paparazzi snapping away with their cameras. The resemblance to Princess Diana's death was not a coincidence.

Banksy's Ciderella chariot crash was both heartbreaking and profound; but Nudelman (writing in businessinsider.com) hints in his article that Banksy's work is 'entertainment' rather than serious 'art'.

In total 58 artists exhibited with other exhibits including:

- *riot model village* by Jimmy Cauty, including 3,000 riot police in the aftermath of civil unrest in urban London;
- *pocket money loans shop* offering loans to children with an interest rate at 5,000% as outlined in its (very) small print;
- *model boat pond* complete with overly crowded boats full of asylum seekers which you could steer by remote control;
- *a* Star Wars *storm trooper* who sulked around the site in misery.

Even to enter the site one was subjected to an extreme form of security: an airport-style screening but with everything made of cardboard. Visitors walked through flimsy cardboard metal detectors under the watchful eyes of security guards and oversized CCTV cameras. There were cardboard rifles on the wall, cardboard walkie-talkies on the table, and a huge sign showing all the many things that were prohibited, under the sarcastic sign "welcome". From the ceiling hung a 'danger – high voltage' sign.

Staff were not there to help and remained uninterested and detached. Their pink high visibility jackets had the word 'dismal' on their backs, and the most you might get from them is a dreary 'welcome to Dismaland'. The visitor was not made to feel comfortable or welcome – I guess that's the whole point.

By the time you read this book the attraction will be long gone, but out of interest it was open from 22nd August to 27th September 2015, from 11am to 11pm, with an admission charge of £3. Though the under 5s got in for free, signs proclaimed that the place was "unsuitable for small children". High demand for tickets caused the Dismaland website to crash repeatedly, causing many to claim that this was a deliberate addition to the Dismaland experience.

As Brown, writing in the Guardian, says: "It is so cool. It is just amazing having this much sarcasm in one place".

Dismaland is located in the old Tropicana lido on Marine Parade, Weston-super-Mare. The town is south-west of Bristol on the M5, which in turn connects to the M4 to London. By train from London change at Bristol Temple Meads. But by the time you read this, Dismaland, as elusive as Banksy himself, will be gone!

Idea for the Classroom: Design your own Theme Park

If you could design your own theme park, what would your theme be? What would you put in it? Most theme parks have a number of areas or zones with a different aspect of the theme in each. For example, a children's theme park might have a zoo, a fun fair, an area based on cartoon characters, and an area themed on food. If your theme were sport then you might have zones dedicated to football, basketball, sporting world records and so on.

Once you have decided on your theme and the zones that will go within the park then you need to decide what the visitor can see or do in each area. Perhaps there might be an exhibition, interactive displays, videos, restaurants and shops. At the Welsh

Show Caves in an earlier chapter there was a farm, medieval village, fossil centre and Millennium Circle aswell as the caves themselves. Each area had its own topic and displays.

If you need inspiration for how to plan your theme park, take a look at the map below. This map takes the visitor from the entrance through a number of zones in turn, ending up at the gift shop and exit. Try one of these themes if you like:

- ❖ animals
- ❖ dinosaurs
- ❖ sport
- ❖ food and drink
- ❖ the body
- ❖ cities of the world

Idea for the Classroom: Paint the Animals

Banksy is well known for his animal themes, and his art that I enjoy most involves painting animals (of course animal rights activists don't agree with this!). His 2003 exhibition *Turf War* exhibited several painted animals, whilst his 2006 exhibition *Barely Legal* exhibited an elephant painted in floral fashion.

Look at the two animals below – they look very bare, unpatterned and unpainted. That's where you come in with your decorative skills as you add pattern and colour to each of the animals. You might like to experiment with chess-board, tartan or polka-dot patterns to jazz up your animals!

Idea for the Classroom: Art Auction

In this activity we are going to have a pretend art auction in the classroom. It's probably best to start by showing some pictures of famous artwork such as Sunflowers or the Mona Lisa. Try to get the children to talk about the art using adjectives and description phrases (wonderful, amazing, great, I think it's fantastic, isn't it great? etc) and ask them which they think is the best and why.

Now you can move on to the auction itself. You'll need several photos of famous paintings for this or, more engaging, get the children to produce their own works of art. If you put the pictures in frames (even paper ones) then they will look more authentic.

Put the students in groups and give each group an equal amount of toy money. They can use this money to 'bid' for the artworks as they come up for auction. I've typed out some basic toy money below, in dollars, and the collection includes one "magic dollar" note which might be strategically important if the bidding is fierce.

Compare your purchases at the end, and ask the groups why they liked and bought each picture. You might end the activity by putting all the pictures up as a large wall display – your own gallery!

Design Your Own Theme Park

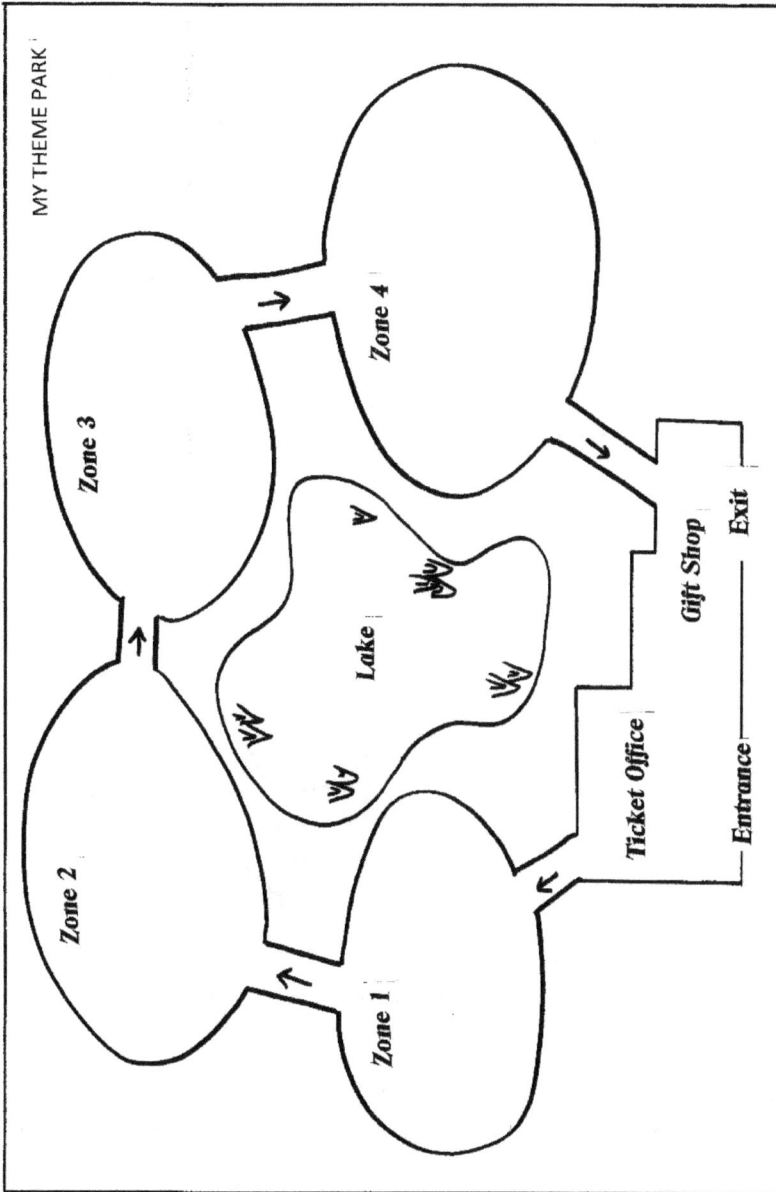

Paint the Animals

PAINT THE ANIMALS

Art Auction Money

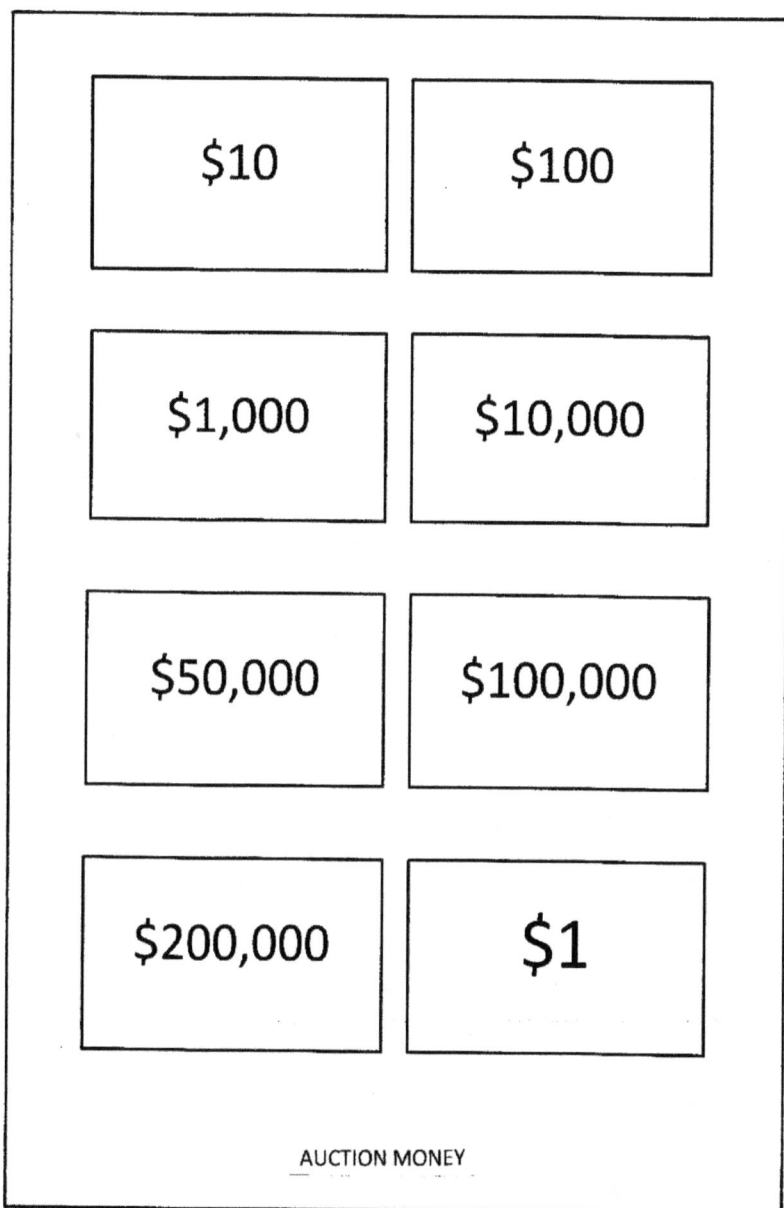

$10	$100
$1,000	$10,000
$50,000	$100,000
$200,000	$1

AUCTION MONEY

BARRY NICHOLSON

12.
THE
EDEN
PROJECT

12.
THE EDEN PROJECT

The Eden Project is a collection of greenhouses, artwork and displays designed to show our relationship to the biological world around us. Located in Cornwall, it has won many awards since opening in 2001.

The former clay pits near St Austell, Cornwall, create an out-of-this-world landscape, like someplace that you'd see in a science fiction movie. Centre stage are two vast biodomes, one replicating a tropical rainforest and the other replicating a Mediterranean environment, and together they form an impressive architectural achievement and, what's more, a showcase of the natural biological diversity of all parts of the world and how humans impact and relate to this natural environment.

The Rainforest Biome is the largest indoor rainforest in the world, housed in a space-age greenhouse measuring 55 metres high and covering a ground area of 3.9 hectares. That means, of course, that they are very large and are home to their own ecosystems and microclimate. The domes when viewed from a distance resemble the eyes of a fly: an interconnecting steel frame filled with what can only be described as large, flat plastic bubbles, mostly hexagonal in shape.

Inside the Rainforest Biome live over 1,000 varieties of plant in four of the earth's rainforest environments: Tropical Islands, South-East Asia, West Africa and Tropical South America. The official Eden brochure promises a 'surprise around every corner' including an Indian sugar truck, painted colourfully and piled high with sugar cane, cocoa plants from which chocolate is made, a full-sized waterfall, and a Malaysian hut complete with paddy field.

The biodome's most famous attraction is the rainforest canopy walkway, allowing visitors to walk on suspended paths high up in the tropical trees. The walkways are fully accessible to the disabled and to children's buggies – indicating the Eden Project's desire to be visitor friendly. The serious side of the walkways and display is that it shows us the importance of rainforests and how they can be used for house building material, fuel, food, clothing and medicine. Indeed, each plant is identified with labels that explain what each can be used for. Wobbly rope bridges with full access and tropical rainstorms are in the planning process.

Next door in the smaller Mediterranean Biodome there is a recreation of that pleasant sub-climate, complete with olive and fruit trees, a vineyard, and thorn and scrub. If you'd like to pretend to be on holiday then eat your lunch at the Med Terrace Restaurant which has a range of local food from pizza to feta cheese salad.

At the centre of the site is the Core, a vast display and exhibition area for all the family. Interactive displays enable visitors to "press buttons, wind handles and peer inside things" according to the official brochure. These exhibits gently educate us about ecosystems, climate change and plant resources. Even the building is designed on the structure of a sunflower and has innumerable solar panels and large ducts that collect rain water ready for re-use.

There is a specially designed children's trail that stretches over the whole site. The idea is that kids have to look for and note down letters that are hidden all over the site, and then form a secret word with the letters. The letters are made of copper and so should, in theory, be easy to find (though you can ask a member of staff for help if you want). I'm sorry, I don't know what the mystery word is, but it is probably something to do with sustainability or ecosystems.

Of course the whole site is built from sustainable resources, and the water collection ducts on the roof of The Core have already been mentioned, and this water is sanitised and used for everything except hand washing and cooking. All on-site electricity is supplied by a nearby wind turbine. If you happen to visit by electric car or bicycle, you can re-charge for free using the charging ports. And arriving by public transport, by bicycle, or walking, gets a discounted entrance fee at the door.

Several special events are held throughout the year. In summer are concerts and a music festival, in the past with performances by Amy Winehouse, Oasis and Elton John amongst others. Summer 2015 has seen *Dinosaur Uproar* – robotic dinosaurs roamed the grounds, and the *Festival of Food* with celebrity chefs showing us how to prepare delicious food. In winter as well as special exhibitions in The Core, there is an ice rink and a Christmas Market.

As an example of how humans can live with nature it is unparalleled, and its emphasis on recycling, biodiversity and use of sustainable resources make it a world leader in demonstrating how we can live an eco life. As one *TripAdvisor* review puts it, the Eden Project and specifically the Rainforest Biodome is a world class entertainment and educational attraction.

As usual there is a visitor centre and gift shop, though it seems a far cry from what was recently available at Stonehenge: in other words, the Eden Project has got its act together – you don't even have to exit through the gift shop! The only problem might be overcrowding with visitors during the busy summer season: apparently one of the biggest challenges is coping with the large number of people visiting, with excess of seven thousand visitors a day at peak. This means queuing for a couple of hours to get in.

But it's worth it, even if it's a little far from London. By car (though you get the feeling they don't really like cars) take the M5 in a south-west direction towards Exeter, then take the A30 until you reach the junction with the A391 from where you can follow the signs. Though there is plenty of car parking space, it might be a long walk or shuttle bus ride to the entrance.

Eden Project prefers it if you visit by public transport, bicycle, or on foot – you get a small discount if you arrive like this. The fast train from London Paddington (on way to Penzance) stops at St Austell and takes about 4½ hours. From St Austell station take the 101 First Bus directly to the main entrance of the site. Apparently you can cycle or walk from Luxulyan railway station (on the Newquay branch line), a distance of about 2.5 miles – and claim your discounted ticket!

You needn't worry about being fed and watered as there are plenty of cafes, a couple of restaurants and a bar on site. Food is eco-friendly and there is a notable lack of fizzy drinks. You may need something stronger than a fizzy drink to recover from the eye-watering entrance fee – even with the discount.

Eden Project is open year-round except Christmas Day; in high summer from 9:30 am to 8 pm with shorter opening hours in winter. On a snowy winter's day it is quite a contrast to walk through the steamy jungle replica and, needless to say, you won't need your winter wardrobe!

Idea for the Classroom: Plant Biodiversity Project

Children love to grow plants from seeds and pips as they can be rewarded with the fruits of their labours as time passes by.

Cress is the easiest and quickest plant to grow, with minimal preparation. Get hold of some cheap plastic plates, a roll of kitchen paper, and some mustard and cress seeds. You'll also need a jug of water. Show the children some photos of plants and flowers and explain to them that they will grow some plants of their own. Give out a plastic plate, a couple of squares of kitchen paper, and some cress seeds to each child. First, lay the kitchen paper over the plate and then scatter the seeds on top. Add a little water – enough to wet the paper and seeds but not drown them – and leave the plate on a shelf at the side of the classroom or take them home. The children should water their cress everyday. Slowly, over the next few weeks, the cress seedlings will grow, until they are ready to add to a salad and eat.

More adventurous and more difficult to grow are tomatoes (great if your school has a vegetable garden) or lemon or orange plants grown from pips, using a clear plastic bag over a flower pot to make a mini-biodome.

Idea for the Classroom: Kid's Trail

Design you own kid's trail, based on the example at the Eden Project, as you hide letters hidden around your classroom, playground or school for your friends to find. First print out some large (A4) bubble letters, one for each letter of your secret word. Good ideas for secret words are ecosystem, biodome, rainforest, or Cornwall. Hide the letters around your 'search area' which ideally is someplace with plants and flowers.

Let's say it's a nice day and you decide to hide the letters around the playground. You can hide one letter up a tree, one on the outside of the building, maybe one underneath where you are sitting to supervise them. Working in groups, the children race to find the letters and note them down. Who can figure out the mystery word first? Below is an example of clues to find the letters:

> The first letter is in the biggest green thing (tree);
> The second letter is near the recycling bin;
> The third letter is near the sweet shop;
> To find the fourth letter you have to score a goal;
> The fifth letter is hidden in the flowers;
> To get the sixth letter you need to look up (school building);
> The seventh letter is in the basket (basketball basket);
> The final letter is under your teacher!

Idea for the Classroom: Planning a Trip to Eden Project

Visiting the Eden Project is not cheap, but most agree that it's worth it. After doing the calculations below, you may agree with those who say it's a once in a lifetime experience. I have compiled a list of prices in the table below (correct as of summer 2015):

Eden Project Tickets and Prices (Summer 2015)

> London Paddington – St Austell
> Adult railway ticket, standard class, single £57
> Adult railway ticket, standard class, return £114
> Child's railway ticket, standard class, single £28.50
> Child's railway ticket, standard class, return £57
> *(Family Rail Card gives 33% discount, not included)*
>
> Entrance
> Adult single ticket £24.75
> Adult single ticket (with 10% discount) £22.50

Family ticket £68.75
Family ticket (with 10% discount) £62.50

Med Terrace Restaurant
Adult pizza £8.50
Child's pizza £5.50
Juices & drinks £3.50 each

Eden Kitchen Restaurant
Roast chicken with salad £7.95
Kid's 'grab a bag' deal £5.95
Juices & drinks £3.50
Exotic ice-cream £2 each

Gift Shop
Recycled Leather Key Ring £1
Kid's Seedling T-shirt (free size) £9.50
Soft Teddy Bear £6.50
Children's guide book £3.50
Tea towel £4.50

Eden Garden Hostel*
1 night for family of four £55
This name has been changed as the hostel is not owned by Eden Project.

Let's give two examples: the first, a family of four (two adults and two children) travelling down by train from London, and who want to eat at an on-site restaurant:

Adult railway ticket, standard class, return £114 × 2 = £228
Child's railway ticket, standard class, return £57 × 2 = £114
Eden Project Family Ticket (includes 10% discount) £62.50
Med Terrace Restaurant 2 × adult pizza £8.50 × 2 = £17.00
2 × children's pizza 5.50 × 2 = £11
4 juices £3.50 × 4 = £14

Gift Shop purchases: 2 children's T-shirts £9.50 × 2 = £19
Children's guide book £3.50
One night for family of 4 at Eden Hostel £55
Note that the adults didn't but anything in the gift shop for themselves, nor did they have any drinks at the bar (!); the stay at the Eden Hostel includes breakfast.
Grand total £524

The second example, a local couple who choose to cycle with their electric bikes to the site and bring their own picnic:

Cycle to site and electric bike re-charge: free
Eden Project Adult Ticket (includes 10% discount) £22.50 ×2 = £45
Gift Shop purchases: Tea Towel £4.50
Note that the couple brought their own food and drink, and bought only a souvenir tea towel from the gift shop. Parking and re-charge of the electric bikes was free.
Grand total: £49.50

A lot of the points are debatable – the couple's picnic might have included smoked salmon sandwiches and champagne (and cost more than the entrance fee); the family could have used a Family Railcard and got a 33% discount, or gone back on the same day and slept on the train avoiding the cost of staying in the hostel; in other words you could skew the grand totals to show exactly the opposite! Putting these unusual situations aside, it is intended that these two examples represent the most or least the average visitor would spend – the reality is most likely somewhere in the middle.

How about your plan for a trip to the Eden Project? Imagine you want to visit with a group of friends, so you need to decide how you are going to get there, what attractions you would like to see, and what you'd like for lunch. Write out an itinerary (time plan) like my examples above, and calculate the grand total.

References

Loch Ness Monster: Real or Fake?

Cambridge Online Dictionary
dailymail.co.uk
jacobite.co.uk
livescience.com
nesie.co.uk
The Times *Loch Ness Monster Hunter Concludes: It's a Big Catfish,* 16th July 2015

King Henry VIII and his Six Wives

hrp.org.uk
Nash, R. 1983, *Hampton Court: The Palace and the People*, Macdonald & Co
Newbery, E. 2006, *Power Palace: Tales From Hampton Court*, Historical Royal Palaces
Royston, A. 1999, *The Six Wives of Henry VIII*, Pitkin Publishing
Underwood, P. 1971, *The A-Z of British Ghosts*, Chancellor Press

The Forth Bridge

coinwiki.co.uk
forthbridgesfestival.com
forth-bridge.co.uk
forth-bridges.co.uk/forth-bridge.html
networkrail.co.uk/Forth-Bridge-repainting-finally-complete.aspx
networkrail.co.uk/Virtual/Archive/forth-bridge
royalmint.com
Wikipedia

The London Underground

20thcenturylondon.org.uk/bech-henry-harry
Ackroyd, P. 2011, London Under, Chatto & Windus
bbc.co.uk/news/uk-20968919 *London Underground Celebrates 150th Anniversary*, 10th January 2013
ltmuseum.co.uk

Martin, A. 2012 Underground Overground: A Passenger's History of the Tube, Profile
tfl.gov.uk
theguardian.com/uk/series/150-years-of-the-underground *The London Underground: A Condensed History*, 9th January 2013
Unknown, 1997, British History: Imperial Britain 1837-1914, Kingfisher Publishing

The Welsh Show Caves

breconbeacons.org
dayoutwiththekids.co.uk
showcaves.co.uk
swcc.org.uk
tripadvisor.co.uk
visitwales.com
wales-underground.org.uk

Thomas Becket

britainexpress.com
catholic.org
eyewitnesshistory.com
historylearningsite.co.uk
schoolhistory.co.uk
Wikipedia

St Crispin and Henry V

Cunningham, G.P. October 25th 2011 *Celebrating St. Crispin's Day*
gonderzone.org/Library/Knights/crispen.htm
shmoop.com
sparknotes.com/Shakespeare/henryv/section9.rhtml
stcrispinsdaynightride.co.uk
themillions.com/2011/10/celebrating-st-crispin's-day.html

Hadrian's Wall

Birley, B. 2004, Junior Activity Guide to Roman Vindolanda, Roman Army Museum Publications
Burton, A. 2007 Hadrian's Wall Path, Aurum Press Ltd
Johnson, J.S. 1990, Chesters Roman Fort, English Heritage
Moffat, A. 2008 The Wall: Rome's Greatest Frontier, Birlinn
Visithadrianswall.co.uk/explore/ad122-hadrians-wall-country-bus

A Tale of Two Dragons

bbc.co.uk
case-coffee.com
historic-uk.com
historytoday.com
resources.woodlands-junior.kent.sch.uk
thewelshdragon.co.uk
walesonline.co.uk
Wikipedia

Stonehenge: Circles in Stone

english-heritage.org.uk
Hill, R. 2008 Stonehenge, Profile Books

Banksy's Dismaland

biography.com
businessinsider.com *Banksy's Dismaland is Art About Nothing – And We're Over It* Nudelman, M. 24th August 2015
dismaland.co.uk
independent.co.uk *Dismaland: The Artists Doing Cooler Things than Banksy at His 'Bemusement Park'*, Wyatt, D. 26th August 2015
streetatrbio.com
theguardian.com *Banksy's Dismaland: Amusementsa and Anarchism in Artists Biggest Project Yet Brown*, M. 20th August 2015
thisiscolossal.com
Wikipedia

The Eden Project

cornwall-online.co.uk
edenproject.com
eden-project.co.uk/eden-story.html
visitcornwall.com
tripadvisor.com
theguardian.com *Take the Kids to… Eden Project, near St Austell, Cornwall*, Choat, I. 18th August 2015

ABOUT THE AUTHOR

Born and educated in the United Kingdom, Barry Nicholson holds a Master's degree in Teaching English as a Foreign Language from the University of Reading. During his career abroad, he has taught in the Far East, Germany, Turkey and Poland. His first book 'Practical English Summercamp Activities' was published in June 2015, followed later that year by 'Famous Tales From Turkey'. He now lives in Krakow, Poland.

From the same author

Practical English Summercamp Activities

Starhands Publishing June 2015

ISBN: 9780993243806

If you want to ensure your students are not just parroting the right answers but actually absorbing the lessons you're teaching them, then allow educator Barry Nicholson to reveal his proven educational method:

ACTIVE FUN + LEARNING = SUCCESS

Whether you're teaching English as a foreign language or working with students who have special needs, this book provides you with more than one hundred enjoyable ways to engage your students in the classroom. Better yet, each activity leaves room for your own creative adjustments and can be adapted to fit your lessons.

Student participation is essential in any educational environment, and with this invaluable resource, you can make learning fun and easy for you and your students!

From the same author

Famous Tales From Turkey With Activities For The Primary Classroom

Starhands Publishing July 2015

ISBN: 9780993243813

Most of us have heard of the Wooden Horse of Troy, Saint Nicholas, or King Midas and his golden touch. But do you know that they all come from what is modern day Turkey?

Educator Barry Nicholson shares twelve tales from Turkey's long and rich history, designed to enliven your class or project work.

Each unit can be used on its own or as a starting point for further study. There are three suggested activities at the end of each section, designed to link the stories to practical activities for the classroom.

The activities bring the tales to life and encourage children to engage with the story.

BARRY NICHOLSON

www.ingramcontent.com/pod-product-compliance
Lightning Source LLC
Chambersburg PA
CBHW071855020426
42331CB00010B/2531